THE PLIMSOLL LINE: COLLECTED ESSAYS AND TALES OF LOVE AND OTHER SUBJECTS

BY GUS UDO

Copyright © 2013 by Augustine F. Udo

All rights reserved. No part of this publication may be reproduced or transmitted in any form or by any means, electronic or mechanical, including photocopy, recording, or any information storage and retrieval system, without permission in writing from the publisher.

Requests for permission to make copies of any part of the work should be submitted to: gusudo@gusudo.com.

The Plimsoll Line: Collected Essays and Tales of Love and Other Subjects/ Gus Udo

1. Essays. 2. Harvard. 3. Humor. 4. Satire. I. Title.

ISBN: 978-0-9840453-3-4

eISBN: 978-0-9840453-2-7

Printed in the United States

First Edition

Dedicated to Isabel and Nicholas

My constant fountains of inspiration

Contents

Preface 4
    ESSAYS 5
English Accent—Good luck with that!..............................1
Crossing the Line 4
The Taxi Driver...12
Economics of Life and Happiness 16
The Transit Point 20
School Days 24
Scoundrels, Bonuses and Bounders 28
Gun Country...33
Mental Health 37
Finding True Love in New York 40
Gym Membership...44
Single Dad—A Typical Kids Weekend 46
Harvard Reunion 51
Saying Goodbye...54
An American Tragedy 59
Entrepreneurship 62
Spooks on the Line..65
Promises—A Weekend in the Country 68
Londris—Europe's Cool New City 78
Africa's Waking Giant—Where Next?............................82
Dharma (Moral Imperative) 88
    TALES 93
Isabella 95

Parisian Tales—You Still Don't Smoke! 99

Portmanteaus..102

The Countessa 105

Ageism..108

The Overcoat 110

    ACKNOWLEDGEMENTS 112

    Acknowledgements...113

    SUGGESTED READING 114

    Suggested Reading 115

    Author's Biography..120

Preface

George Orwell in his marvelous book, *Why I Write*, offers up four key reasons why authors pen their work: 1) Sheer egotism 2) Aesthetic enthusiasm 3) Historical impulse and 4) Political purpose. I would add a number 5), because it is a Refuge from the outside world. Writing undoubtedly provides a safe if exhausting haven from other more worldly distractions. I would rank 1) 4) and 3) as my key driving forces. There is something delightful about squeezing thoughts out from your brain onto paper hopefully in coherent readable form for others to share and perhaps enjoy. It's a very powerful impulse, to share your thoughts with your fellow beings in a deliberate thoughtful way. Similarly, in a world where there is so much wrong and where inequality is rampant, writing provides a forceful means of non-violent expression. There is also the lure of history, the desire to craft a legacy either in the form of a literary estate or as a means of effecting change. Finally, perhaps my writing is also a simple matter of capturing a moment in time for posterity.

ESSAYS

English Accent—Good luck with that!

Invariably, the first question I am asked when people meet me is: "Where is your accent from?" Or "where are you from?" This happened to me yesterday. The question was posed, on this particular occasion, by a Brooklyn native. I volleyed back at her in my best BBC English, "My accent is from England, but where I am from is a little more complicated," I knew it was time once again to deliver my brief *précis* on American linguistic history. It starts like this. "You realize that the Mayflower Pilgrims had English accents?" My comments were predictably met with a dumfounded look. "The Pilgrims spoke English with Shakespearean pronunciation. In fact, most of the early settlers had English accents, even the founding fathers like George Washington and John Adams."

"Really, they had English accents!"

"Yes," I eagerly responded. Silence ensued; my curious inquisitor appeared lost for words. I continued. "An English accent was not an impediment to the Pilgrims becoming American. In fact, how much more authentic can an American be than arriving in Massachusetts with an accent from the same place as the founding fathers?" As the wise judge told all assembled at my naturalization swearing-in ceremony, in downtown Manhattan, on a frigid December morning almost two decades ago, "You are now an American like any other American born in the United States; don't let anyone under any circumstances tell you otherwise." I woke up that morning as an "alien" with a Green Card and left the ceremony with the proud glow of a fully fledged American.

I made a conscious decision to come to America almost thirty-five years ago. This profound journey to citizenship sets me and others like me apart from those that inherited the privilege of being called Americans. Granted, unlike the Pilgrims, I was spared a harrowing Atlantic Ocean crossing in a crowded, disease ridden three-masted Galleon, furled sails tumbled loose by the fury of heavy seas, gigantic waves threatening to end it all. There was no pestilence awaiting me in America. I did not encounter hostile natives eager to defend their shores from foreign accented invaders. My welcome to America, for the most part, was cordial.

Now many years later, despite living on the eastern seaboard of the United States for almost thirty years, in fact most of my adult life, I still cling desperately to my proper English accent. It is an asset that I treasure and maintain with great pride, even more so as an American. Periodic trips to London ensure my diction remains fluid and encompasses the medley of intriguingly nuanced and often humorous social trends that drive language and its use in England. For instance, there are the many meanings of the word "tackle." Tackle can refer to fishing equipment, a football (soccer) challenge, or male unmentionables, depending on context.

My London accent baffles the English as much as it does my fellow Americans. I do not speak in the unaccented American English twang they are accustomed to hearing from an American. My English accent comes from where I grew up and not from my country of origin. No doubt the Pilgrims would have expressed the same bewilderment and curiosity at the accents of other subsequent arrivals to the New World from elsewhere.

I hope my accent serves as an inspiration and a reminder for those yet to come to this country—a reminder that Americans have, since the country's founding, hailed from far and wide. And have spoken English with many accents, perhaps something not all Americans necessarily want to be reminded of.

Recently on a taxi ride in the Hudson Valley, a blithe taxi driver enquired:

"Are you from across The Pond?" Looking up from checking my text messages, I congratulated him:

"Wow, you have a very keen ear for accents."

"Almost everything sounds better spoken with an English accent," he replied breezily with eager excitement. Judging from the many American television advertisements nowadays that feature English accents, his observations must have more than a modicum of truth. Anything said in an English accent sounds intelligent. There is probably well known empirical studies on the matter that have escaped my attention. Although I have never regarded my accent as a commercial asset, I am glad there are those who consider me smart simply by virtue of my dulcet tones.

The cabdriver's observation however, has not always been my reality. My accent usually results in wrong restaurant orders being delivered to my table or taxi rides to unplanned destinations—e.g., Queen's Village in Queen's Borough New York, instead of Greenwich Village in Manhattan. In that momentary lapse connecting visage and accent, New York cabdrivers miss the crucial beat required to accurately process my words, which in turn, renders my directions meaningless. Likewise at the post office, mundane activities, like buying stamps can turn into the most complicated ordeal.

The combination of my African face and an English accent appears until recently to have been a revelation for some of my fellow Americans. They have no idea that Black Britons, (which I technically am not), actually have, well, English accents just like the Mayflower Pilgrims and founding fathers.

Crossing the Line

Each time I visit London, I am struck at how couples there, seemingly very different from each other in almost all ways you can imagine, are attracted to each other. In London's Bayswater recently, I saw an unlikely couple entering a London Black Cab, a Middle Eastern woman in traditional head-to-toe black garb and a man (presumably Scottish) clad in a Stewart Tartan Kilt and sporran. They seemed very much in love and happy with each other despite their external differences. I've often pondered the complexities of mixed unions; the varieties in which they can be found and the secrets of their success.

Growing up as a child, a mixed union meant a marriage outside of our kinship group in the town of Onitsha, Nigeria, our ancestral family home. Such marriages required thick skin and the ability to endure the many slights and barbs that would be thrown your way for crossing the line. The prying eyes and wagging tongues of village gossips would be unleashed. Those who followed convention and married Onitsha-Ibos generally met with instant approval. They also enjoyed the practical benefits of a spouse who spoke the same language with shared values and traditions. Such marriages took place between men and women from outside their respective villages, presumably to maintain the integrity of the town's gene pool. Marriage *"outside"* the sixteen villages that make up Onitsha was considered taboo and an abrogation of the tight cultural bounds that define an Onitsha person. Consequences of *"marrying outside"* were evident in my family where my paternal grandfather did the unthinkable and married an Ibo princess from another nearby town. Under native custom, this transgression excluded my father from being able to contest the democratic right to kingship within the Onitsha community. This was a grave matter for him and a source of some consternation. There was no way to fix his flawed ancestral line within the Onitsha context. My father was a polygamist, and took great care to ensure that his three wives were from Onitsha, so the same fate would not befall his children—even if they hadn't the vaguest interest in contesting Onitsha kingship. In Onitsha, all the indigenous families within the town know each other. Through oral tradition they even track hereditary traits, e.g., obesity, tallness, arthritis, or mental illness generationally in families. As a result, individuals have a strong sense of the families they are marrying into. In Onitsha they say you marry a family not just the bride or groom. Everyone knows the rules of dating and marriage. And while there are no arranged marriages, per se, there is a keen awareness of which families would provide suitable matches.

Before I was six-years old, in 1965, we moved and lived in each of the three regions that comprised Nigeria. In each region we discovered the cultural diversity of Nigeria and its multiplicity of tribal groups. There are over three hundred languages and dialects. We also learned about another type of mixed union; unions that went a step further beyond Ibo communities, across tribal and linguistic lines. In some cases this also involved crossing religious boundaries if combinations were between southern Christians—Ibos or Yoruba—and northern—Hausa-Fulani—who were Muslims. Partners in Hausa-Fulani unions would likely have to contend with polygamy, which was far more frequent in the northern part of the country. Wives would no longer have the rights and protection afforded under their own native custom as women. Their rights were now in the provenance of the traditions and practices of Nigeria's centuries old Muslim community. Such unions were a relatively rare phenomenon then and a cause of local scandal. However, some Onitsha women are known to have happily married men from the North, usually wealthy ones. A cousin of my father's ended up leaving Onitsha, and Nigeria altogether to become one of several wives of the mayor of Douala in the Cameroon.

Marriages across tribal lines in many respects faced much stiffer obstacles in terms of acceptance because of some of the deep-rooted enmities in those days among the three dominant tribes, which surfaced in the country's civil war in 1967. The bloody three-year Biafran conflict placed tremendous strain and challenges on many mixed unions that had crossed tribal lines. Many, driven by deep love, and against all odds survived while others were pulled asunder by the national conflict that saw neighbor fighting neighbor. In order to survive, many of those involved in mixed unions found sanctuary abroad in England, France, Germany and America, during the war. These were places in which their ethnic or religious differences were not a matter of life and death.

Over time forward thinking families crossed rigid barriers in order to marry into prominent families from other tribal groups. This meant that these families were able to build networks that were national or even transnational in character, similar to unions in the British aristocracy. One of Nigeria's former (now late) Supreme Court Judges and Ad-hoc Judge at the International Court of Justice in The Hague was a case in point having married a European. These were mostly love matches among the country's elite, who met at the nation's prestigious schools and through social events.

The first time I came across a black-white mixed union was one of my father's work colleagues who had married an American woman from a liberal intellectual family in the early 1960s. The couple and their children were seen as very exotic and people were not quite sure of what to make of them. One can only imagine how the marriage would have been received in the US at that time. Prior to that, the only white people I had known were clerics and nuns. Then my mother's cousin, a UK trained doctor, married an Englishwoman which meant that new grounds had been broken within our immediate family. These marriages from what I understood worked relatively well within the local culture. The outsiders were for the most part embraced and assimilated into the community. They ate local food and learned to tie native wrappers and headscarves that are the traditional dress in eastern Nigeria. Many of these newcomers learned the language and customs and took part in most aspects of community life. These foreign wives naturally missed their families abroad. Those who could afford to spent time in their homelands with their children during holidays.

Some sent their children to English, French or Swiss boarding schools. Many of their children continue to live in Nigeria today and have intermarried locally. I might add that there were also European men married to locals, but I am less familiar with these pairings.

When we moved to London in 1966 to escape the country's civil war, we found for the first time another type of mixed union—that of Nigerians marrying men or women from the West Indies. These matches met with hostility from my parents' generation who saw a chasm between the values and identities of the two cultures. This was also a period during which there was furious competition for jobs between Caribbean and African professionals and other qualified immigrants in England. Because of the unenlightened stigma of slavery among some, this was the least favored of all mixed unions by Onitsha indigenes.

Living in Sixties London with cosmopolitan parents and a father who was at best ambivalent about the viability of mixed unions outside of the Onitsha community, dating was challenging in our household. Although we were for all intents and purposes cut-off from Onitsha society in Nigeria and had only a relatively small group of families among which to socialize and marry, father still insisted that we maintain family tradition. This backdrop made dating local English girls a major event in our household. At seven, I was too young for these matters to be of consequence but for my teenage elder brother and sister, these issues loomed large. My father's tight grip on the household loosened when he found a new job and was transferred back to Nigeria after he had lost his senior post at Nigeria Airways because we were Ibos—the enemy in the Biafran conflict.

Unlike foreign wives that settled in Nigeria, the onus was on us to learn the odd ways of the English and their oscular courting habits—e.g., making-out in public (*snogging* in British English). As I became a teenager and began to date locally it became apparent that I would have to navigate the delicate gap between our Nigerian customs and English sensibilities. I generally did not invite dates to our home since these issues of culture were simply too awkward to explain. Like why guests are welcomed by breaking kola nuts and why titled guests receive theirs first and thereafter other guests in descending order of age. It required a very well rounded and mature individual to understand the limits of Onitsha social customs and their touch points with English culture. Also, I did not have the vocabulary to even begin to explain such limits. The girls I dated for the most part were Catholic, which made life somewhat easier since at least we were not crossing religious barriers. The parents of my first serious girlfriend, a lovely redheaded Irish young lady went out of their way to make me welcome. I sensed that they understood what it was like to be an outsider. There were many Irish missionaries in Nigeria, and no doubt they reported back that we were agreeable people and perhaps even good company.

At the time there was an undercurrent of racism pervasive in the UK, particularly in popular culture. The Black and White Minstrel Show was still a regular feature on television and *Golliwogs* were emblazoned on jars of Robinson's Marmalade. Black consciousness or indeed London's vaunted multiculturalism simply did not exist in the bucolic confines of suburban Mill Hill in London's Green Belt; you blended in as best you could. It was not like inner London, where different types of people of various colors, looks, and traditions lived cheek to jowl, all jumbled up together in the same tightly woven neighborhoods. As a result, life in my teenage years was largely cloistered from the tensions of mixed unions. This may have also been helped by the fact that I was a scholar-athlete of some local repute having been selected to compete for Great Britain and England in track and field. This local celebrity status may have placed more favorable light on me as a datable match.

It was not until I came to college in America that the racial, cultural and religious dimensions of mixed dating became truly apparent to me. Having experienced a multicultural London, I was surprised at the monolithic stereotyping that abounded on campus. This was very different from the America I had imagined where barriers were invisible. The schisms and the rules which dedicated invisible lines between, WASPs, Jocks, Preps, LA and New York types, African-Americans, Jews, Irish Catholics and Bostonians and other New Englanders were all new to me. So new in fact, that throughout my four years at Harvard, I never really knew exactly how to distinguish between all the different groups. I discovered that some African-American classmates were reluctant to date an African. Some found that I was not "black enough," meaning not sufficiently attuned to the black experience in America. I heard this theme echoed years later while on dates with a very charming African-American stage and screen actress. It took me many years to understand what they were saying, which now as a full-fledged American of color, I can certainly appreciate. Mercifully, there were also those who were curious to date me and found my African and English combination alluring. I dated across white and black color lines but not without some discomfort on both sides. One time, an attractive flirtatious Asian-American upper classmate approached me, and seemed interested to be my *squeeze*. She asked if I liked Asian girls but I had no real sense at the time what dating a Korean-American would be like. Smart and spunky, she was intrigued that our family names were very similar. But I was having enough challenges dating so-called regular Americans—both black and white. I declined her approach. I remember her saying, "You don't get it do you"—meaning the comfort that comes with being with someone else with the same outsider perspective. In hindsight I now recognize exactly what she meant.

Outside of college, I have found it much harder to find and date either African or African-Americans who are my peers, in part because of demographics on the small island of Manhattan. I also don't quite fit neatly into the box in either orthodoxy, not being fish or fowl. I am sure a small town mid-Westerner that grew up in

Zambia might feel the same about dating somebody from say Mobile, Alabama—a place I have had the rare privilege of visiting.

Girlfriends I have dated in New York have been mostly multicultural. I remember an elder Egyptian gentleman, a night doorman at the mid-town bachelor apartment where I lived at the time. He would glance at my dates, giving an approving nod or tut-tutting and grimacing while fiddling with his prayer beads. Like a father or guardian angel, he always had a look of apprehension when he thought I had wondered too far, so to speak from my roots. After a succession of "tut-tut" dates, African-American, white-American, Cape Verdean (Island off the West Coast of Africa), Swedish, Korean-American, Brazilian-Japanese, and Guyanese (but raised partly in Nigeria) his face finally lit up signaling approval. Unfortunately, the petite, elegant young lady, a Wall Street lawyer, did not share his view.

I have encountered ugly racial bias from close family members of some white-American girlfriends, as well as isolated hostility from within the African-American community. This I have found somewhat ironic. During my early days in New York, in the 1990s, some New Yorkers of both racial persuasions were not shy to share their contrary views on the situation with my date and me. One time, I went to see a slave history documentary with a white-American date, and as we left the movie house a young perfectly normal looking African-American man waved for me to come over. He whispered in my ear looking at my date over my shoulder, "Haven't you learned anything from the movie?" He then walked away without fanfare or rancor.

I can't say that color drives my dating choices, like most people, circumstance plays a big role in who you meet and are attracted to. I do wish however that New York had more of a cultural vibrancy that was truly inclusive—one that sees and understands that we have similarity in our differences, like the disarming Bayswater couple.

The Taxi Driver

I met a Black Taxi Cab driver in London who lived for six months of the year driving his cab and three months living wild, half-naked in the trees in the forests of England, or so he claimed. We chatted at length as he drove me from Paddington station to my hotel in *the City*—London's financial district. London Cabbies are renowned for their chattiness and large brains. The latter is attributed to the demands of passing "The Knowledge," an ancient examination that requires Cabbies to know intimately London's medieval road network.

"Where are you visiting from?" He asked curiously, sizing me up in his rear view mirror. The red courtesy signal light in the back of the cab was on which meant he could hear through the connected microphone and speaker intercom whatever noises were coming from the back seats.

"New York!" I said.

"I went there once but it was too fast. Too many lights and cars for my taste and worse still, your yellow cabs are a joke. Geezer driving my girlfriend Jo and I, didn't speak English and didn't know where he was going."

"It's a lovely place," I said looking to defend the charms of my transplanted home.

"That it may be but not for me, mate. I've been driving my cab for 20 years. Park it at home for three months each year so me and Jo can go and live half-naked in the forest with our friends."

"Now that's bloody amazing, mate!"

"We forage for food and wash in the river. We sleep in tree hammocks rain or shine. Fortunately the summer weather the last few years has been kind. If the weather in England were better, we'd

The Taxi Driver

live like that all year round. Instead we go to *Benidorm*—in Spain—during the winter where we have a house for another three months before coming back for six months during which I drive my cab."

"That sounds very agreeable," I said. "Tell me, how do you manage to have so much time off?"

"Got kids, but they're all grown up now, so we do what we want when we want. Besides, they spend most of their time with their mum."

"Sounds amazing," I reiterated enthusiastically, not knowing whether he was winding me up or not, although the excitement in his voice led me to believe he was telling the truth. George—that was his name—went on to say that time in seclusion in the forest clears the mind of cobwebs and liberates the soul.

"Your mind is cleansed of junk. You experience clarity about life and its worth I can't even begin to describe. A breath of fresh air!" He sucked in the air in his cab though flared, horse-like nostrils. I noted quietly to myself that the musty air in the cab for sure couldn't have been as invigorating as that in the forest.

As a consequence, he continued, he didn't read newspapers and was extremely careful what sources of news he allowed to pollute his brain.

"Its like food; if you eat rubbish it will have a consequence on your health and quality of life. News is the same; avoid junk, if you want to stay healthy. Would you knowingly put rotten molding food in your mouth?"

He quickly answered his rhetorical question, "Of course not! Then why would you let yourself be consumed by moldy news?"

His simple but elegant maxim seemed to have merit. Peering at the driver's face, I saw that he looked tanned and a picture of health. His blonde dreadlocks, streaked with grey flecks, floated up and down from the wind entering the cab window and rested gently on his broad tattooed forearms. His features gave no hint of his fifty years, which he had earlier revealed as we crossed the Blackfriars Bridge. I verified George's age by cross-referencing various events as we talked, like the Queen's Silver Jubilee celebrated back on June 7, 1977. It was a memorable day for schoolboys and girls in England. We were about the same age, give or take a few months, and facts of such an event, like the street parties, were unlikely to be recounted in vivid detail by someone who did not live the occasion.

George's observation about the news resonated with me and I paused to reflect. The old adage that some London Cabbies are masterminds might well be true after all. George pressed on through London's heavy traffic. The steady rattle of his diesel engine could be heard as we stopped at each traffic light. He continued to philosophize, explaining that the pernicious influence of the press has grown even more sinister with the arrival of the internet age. "The public are lazier than ever," he declared.

"Headlines are rarely truthful mate, whether it's football or politics. They are designed to sell news and not necessarily the truth. It's only when you read or listen or watch further that you notice the headline may not match the substance of the story. Its even worse now with the internet, where you get lots of snippets of news."

I was a convert. In an age where time is precious, few are discerning or curious enough to linger to ponder the links between what is reported and what is reality. Obtaining accurate news often requires digging and sifting across the Internet and other traditional media sources.

It suddenly occurred to me this day in this cab that mind clutter is the bane of modern existence. It's a yolk, which inhibits creative and productive thought, and vital enriching human interaction. As George pointed out:

The Taxi Driver

"I am even mindful of them social media internet bots (robots) things. You know the bots that trawl news stories and generate automated Twitter responses that mimic human beings." These bots, one understands, are used frequently, particularly around major elections, to influence political dialogue.

"Electronic Internet bots masquerading as paramours now plague even dating sites!" George exclaimed and began to laugh out loud as he sped on with dreadlocks flowing in the breeze. We were finally at my hotel. George's parting remarks were: "Mark my words; avoiding ingesting junk is mandatory if you want to stay sane and healthy. It's a very complex matter when it comes to news and media today, mate!" He sped off again, ready to amuse and inform his next fare.

Since my brief cab episode with the feral but professorial George, I've grown much more discerning about the news I consume. BBC and NPR feature heavily on my menu. I take great care nowadays to filter out irrelevant news that clogs the mind and adds little to one's knowledge and understanding of the world. I am now a fast and firm follower of the Georgian approach to news. I also have a new-found regard for those who choose to dwell in trees. I may well explore whether a summer semi-naked in the wilderness is a worthy goal for me—if only to have the enlightened clarity of thought that George exhibited—what Germans term *Imkaltenkellernebenmuffigenkoffernwehfreude*.

Economics of Life and Happiness

In case you didn't notice, New York represents one of the global bastions of a material culture. Friends in New York look aghast when I reveal that I have no interest in money beyond having sufficient funds for basic incidentals, occasional travel and other crucial obligations including taxes. I do not own a house, condo/coop, car, yacht, jet, or holiday villa, although I will confess to owning a bicycle. I was also once the proud owner of a rather nice coop apartment and I still own part of a business I founded more than a quarter of a century ago. I am the wrong person to ask the question, "What's your favorite car?" I have never owned a car my entire life, which seems to come as a great surprise to some. I rarely drive, perhaps once every ten years. To answer the question in your head at this point, No, I do not live off the capital from my inheritance unless you are referring to my wits. My waning interest in the material trappings of life was triggered by my separation from the mother of my children, after almost 15 years together. The acrimonious split was sufficient to acquaint me with the negative qualities of money. My diminished interest in material possessions should therefore not be equated with resignation or with aspirations to be an ascetic. I like the good things in life as much as the next man or woman—in moderation of course.

The intangibles, happiness and time, have been at the center of a life reexamined for me, to find my psychic as opposed to fiscal net worth. Meaning in life for me is paramount. Being bereft of unnecessary material things has been strangely liberating. It's forced me to focus on my real needs and to ask what money is, as well as a great many other questions about the matrices in life that make for happiness. I've always considered myself enormously wealthy, being blessed with the extraordinary love of a goodly number of family and friends. Money seems meaningless by comparison, particularly since it is usually to be found at the center of contention in many unpleasant situations. I recognize that at the other extreme, an abundance of money can make for a materially easier life without worries about children's school fees and college tuition. It can also inspire individuals to perform extraordinary acts of unparalleled human generosity. Money certainly helps in life to provide vital basics such as food, clothing, shelter, health care, education and the occasional vacation to refresh body and soul. We live in a society that tells us that we need much more than this to be happy. My own view is that this is a myth. I've found myself in recent times much happier with fewer material things. You would be surprised how many New Yorkers think that money and glossy *things* are a plausible substitute for happiness. I certainly don't measure myself by money or possessions. It's simply not my gauge of success in life. This view runs counter to the daily onslaught to consume and spend in the epicenter of the material world, aka New York City. This prompted me, while recently contemplating the juxtaposition of the necessity of work and the import of happiness, to briefly consider a life without money! Something that is easier said than done. Unless, that is, you enter a religious order and undertake a vow of poverty, and give up money entirely. This radical course would compel you to be more tethered to the immeasurable comfort and generosity of community, if only for survival. Unfortunately, it still leaves the practical unanswered problem of how to fiscally and emotionally support and nurture one's offspring in the interim. I am not quite ready for this drastic step—or indeed, to take to the streets Orwellian style as a vagrant, despite its sartorial appeal. The way forward, may lay in a simple and elegant step backwards—i.e., less time collecting material things and more spent living life.

Time is an exceedingly precious commodity for me, perhaps even more so than money. I remember in school as a teenager in 1970s London discussing in sociology class the merits of the coming of the leisure society. We were told to expect a future where due to new machines and gadgets we would work less and have far more time to enjoy life. The future seemed very bright indeed. Looking at the lives of many of my peers and much of America, the leisure society clearly has not arrived for rich or poor. Americans work too hard. We strive for illusionary material wealth that detracts from the quality of our lives. More emphasis needs to be placed on quality not quantity. I find myself like most New Yorkers perennially racing, rarely stopping to contemplate each day's accomplishments. I have long admired the French for their dogged insistence on maintaining a balance between work, life and play. The French work to live they do not live to work. New Yorkers in contrast are unforgiving and unrelenting in the pursuit of money for an illusionary life a notch or two above their neighbor—*The American Dream*. The singular activity of making tons of money has become a means to itself in some professional circles, e.g., bankers, consultants and lawyers at the expense it seems, of having a life.

How much do we really need to feel safe? Can we benefit from a simpler life? These are important questions given the prevalence of waste in today's society. We certainly can have more with less, as I am learning. Waste pervades every aspect of modern society from our bloated inefficient bureaucracies to New York's court systems where resources are daily squandered on inane lawsuits. Waste is evident in our convenience restaurants where food is piled a mile high, beyond the reasonable appetite of most citizens. Manhattan apartment dwellers in posh neighborhoods open windows wide on the coldest winter days to escape the tyranny of unregulated indoor steam heating. Reason seems to have been lost as we search everywhere to create a notion of wealth. Few people seem to realize that there are more men and women sleeping in shelters and on the streets today in New York than there were during the great depression. We have plenty for everyone. But much of it is wasted or is sucked into the coffers of a few. Inequality—the gap between *haves* and *have nots*—continues to grow at an alarming pace.

There are to my mind attendant burdens and responsibilities to community that come with having money—responsibilities that seem forgotten except by a special few, like a New York restaurateur friend of mine. Over dinner recently she explained that she understood the economics of life for her many employees and their daily tussle for shrinking opportunities. As an offspring of immigrant parents, she was unusually, both sympathetic and empathetic toward the plight of the working poor, blue-collar workers who comprise a good part of her workforce. The quality of their lives is as much a focus for her as her firm's bottom-line. In fact, she sees the two as inextricably entwined.

How you use money is of great significance, which brings us back to the question of life without it. It is hard to function in modern society without money. The challenge or conundrum is to achieve a balance. This is no easy task. Winston Churchill once said, "We make a living by what we get, we make a life by what we give." For those who have money, giving is one solution. Trimming your hours of work and how much you make is another option that seems increasingly popular in Europe among those fortunate enough to still have a job.

The balance between money, life and ambition is a delicate one. Do you park fulfillment in order to chase money? Or do you stay steadfastly focused on the quality of your life and what's required to sustain it? The latter is my choice; balance, sanity and happiness seem so much more appealing than another gadget.

We all need to be given a sufficient sense of worth beyond money. As a French politician once said when comparing France and America, "Here in France we speak of *citizens* not *taxpayers*." My own ambition is not tied to being rich—I want to accomplish so much more than money can buy. Money is not even at the center of my personal motivation to succeed as an entrepreneur, which runs counter to what most perceive as the tenet of today's capitalist society in which I choose to live. I do however recognize the inevitable confluence of commercial success and money and the responsibility, which comes with it.

The Transit Point

In my hazy dream I arrived too early to check-in and was told I would have to wait until guests were checked-out that afternoon. Those bound for hell would be vacating their rooms. There were an unusually large number of guests bound for hell that day so there would be plenty of rooms available mostly with windows nostalgically facing earth. Being New Year's Day, which was the busiest time of the season, the transit point for heaven and hell departures was packed. Travelers ticketed for hell I was told were usually easy to recognize, they were the ones looking unusually grim, solemn with a resigned air of eternal damnation. Many had long given up on God and humanity. Some were making a commotion protesting vociferously that their one-way tickets had been incorrectly labelled. Those with a gaiety about them were in transit for heaven although some passengers have been known to try it on with the authorities by assuming a false air of excitement. The transit staff was trained and well schooled on how to ferret out fakes. Besides, the ticketing system was infallible. Your destination was written on your forehead and would be read automatically by the error-free system employed by the transit vessels. My departure had been scheduled for noon the next day, so I had approximately 24 hours to explore the utilitarian delights of the transit facility.

Next to me was a young man who said he wanted to return to earth since the promised virgins were nowhere to be found. I said perhaps they are waiting for you in heaven but he was unmoved. The young lady seated on my other side fidgeted nervously. She could barely contain her excitement; she said there were so many relatives she was looking forward to seeing. But upon checking the list of those in heaven as against those in hell, she found only a few of her relatives had made it to the coveted destination. There were those of fame whom she was also going to seek out, the likes of historical figures like Florence Nightingale, Mother Teresa, Brutus, Richard Nixon and Salvador Dali. Only Florence and Teresa had made the "Heaven List." Salvador Dali's application, although well presented and fabulously illustrated had been scotched by a new ordinance that forbade entry to those new candidates (male or female), with strange looking mustaches. Tree huggers and hipsters were also excluded. It was easier to get into a top-flight Upper Eastside New York coop or nightspot than it was to get a seat on the heaven express. Those on the heaven express were truly in an exclusive club.

From all accounts everything you can imagine was available in heaven but the lines were inordinately long, like Disney World. But nothing compared to what those destined for hell would be facing. Traffic was reputed to be very heavy in heaven but again nothing compared to what those in hell would be facing. In fact, the sheer weight of numbers of souls from time past permanently in residence in heaven and hell complicated things in both destinations. There was from all accounts no air-conditioning or shade to be found in hell and what food there was, as one might expect, was very bad, as were the beaches. Big data techniques were used to track numbers in great detail but nobody knew exactly how the tracking system worked. Not even Albert Einstein, who apparently was a long time heaven resident along with Archimedes, Galileo and Copernicus, had a clue. Things were further complicated by the fact that cameras and cell phones were not allowed in either place. There was also no fraternization beyond here. Speculation abounded about what heaven and hell were actually like since nobody really knew.

I retired early, weary from my long journey from earth and slept well. Visibility was good when I woke, just in time to enjoy the breathtaking view of earth and the stars in the distant galaxies beyond. I was fortunate enough to have received a room on the upper floors several billion miles in the nothingness of space. The elevator was remarkably fast covering the distance and delivering me to my well-furnished room in the blink of an eye. Some of the rooms, I noticed, were somewhat small and Spartan, but I was lucky.

This was probably due to the fact that all stays were for a single night only without exception, even VIPs for both destinations. Genghis Khan, Hitler, Stalin and Pol-Pot apparently got a little hot under the collar about this and seemed unhappy with their ticketed destination.

The lobby was full of guests that morning checking-in and checking-out. I noticed a group huddled in a corner; someone who looked like Marylyn Monroe appeared to be among them, listlessly drifting. I enquired of one of the transit staff as to who they were. "Oh, you mean the *lost souls*; those are complicated cases whose fate has yet to be decided and may never be resolved. They sleep in the facility; some have been here for nearly an eternity."

My white spotless celestial transit vessel arrived and hovered mysteriously above the boarding point. I checked that the sign on the front was clearly marked "Heaven" and not "Hell," and moved to my designated silo from which I would presumably ascend to the vessel. The silos themselves gave no indication of whether you were destined for heaven or hell. Those waiting for the jet-black transit vessel marked "Hell," in bold large flashing red letters, looked on. Loading was now commencing; and one by one, each soul vanished from the millions of loaded translucent pods. Soon it was my turn.

Is there a God? This is a question that has baffled man since the beginning of time. It's a hugely ambitious topic that's reflective of the fractal nature—stochastic self-similarity—of the world around us and our enquiring minds' need to know. I was brought up as a Roman Catholic and attended Catholic high school. My life however has been largely free of the symbolic practice of active religion. I am a believer in the basic tenets of good and evil that the Church teaches but the mystical dimensions of faith, the Eucharist and its related dogma are antithetical to my own belief.

I do not believe in God. The notion of a supreme being seems too much like a montage of our own making, something concocted by theologians to soothe our curious minds. These views however do not invalidate the importance of belief, prayer and communing for the human psyche. The world can be a frightful place and anything spiritual that makes it more comforting can only be good in so far as it does not impinge on the rights of others to peacefully enjoy their lives. So, yes, I believe in religion but not because of God. Of course one might argue that there is no religion without the existence of God, a view I do not share.

Religion, nevertheless, can also be dangerous. A divisive force, especially when used to fan hatred and discord among people. I am not a religious scholar but my guess is that the basic tenets of Christianity, Buddhism, Judaism, and the Muslim faith all teach tolerance.

So, yes, religion is definitely worth it, if it makes us treat others better. Now back to my journey.

Resigned to my fate my mind was calm. I stood erect dressed in my white hooded transit jump suit, arms relaxed by my side gazing up. The light in my pod flashed a steady urgent red, meaning ready to go. I glanced at the line behind me drifting out beyond infinity of silent transit travelers waiting their turn. At that instance, a beam of light emitted from the transit vessel immersed my pod. I was no more. Some moments later I opened my eyes with great expectation but saw only the malfunction light quietly blinking anti-climatically on the pod console above my face. A second more powerful beam of light followed. In the now empty pod, the console flashed, "TRANSIT COMPLETED."

School Days

It is seven o'clock and mum has already left for work. Capital Radio is blaring outside in the hallway. My older brother is up and the glass front door will slam shut like clockwork at 7:30 am as he leaves for work which will signal time for me to get up and get ready for school. My preferred bus is the 8:10 am. Face washed teeth brushed and school uniform on; I gobble my Shredded Wheat with *Ovaltine* poured on top and race out the door for the bus with my school bag trailing. My younger brother Martin usually tries for the 8:20 am, opting to sleep that additional ten minutes and sometimes skip breakfast. All bus times are approximate, give or take 10 minutes to an hour. This was a very different England from that of today—buses arrived in their own good time irrespective of the timetable, which everyone knew was no more than a glass encased decorative element on the concrete post at the bus stop.

First Bus Stop—The 221 red double-decker routemaster arrives and I board and show my half-pass and pay my fare. The boys who live a few yards down the road show their free school bus passes—I look on with envy. It seems that someone at the local authority, seeing our foreign names has elected not to give us free bus passes, deeming us closer to the school than them. There is a pecking order on the bus for the school children—girls and wimps downstairs with the old grannies. Hopeless tearaways and smokers on the long back seat on the top deck, pretty cool girls at the front upstairs and everyone else in-between.

The pretty and very smart Howard sisters sit at the bottom. They attend St. Michaels, the Catholic sister school to ours where the girls are much brighter than the renegade boys from my school. Cathy Howard is a year older and very quiet and reflective—perhaps a little shy. Emma, a striking English rose, is much more confident and unusually direct. Emma was popular with all the boys though few plucked up the courage to joust with her. I usually smile like a silly goat as I pass Cathy, running to my usual seat upstairs. Their father, if I am not mistaken, was a lecturer, perhaps even at the LSE (The London School of Economics and Political Science). *Billy Liar* style, I indulged in fantasies that perhaps they were related to the Howards of Henry VIII's era. Catherine Howard was Henry VIII's fifth wife; she was referred to as his "rose without a thorn," but when her torn was revealed as a sexual past, she was beheaded. Probably not family history you would be keen to talk about.

My Rastafarian friend Andy Bryan was sometimes on the bus with his ankle length drainpipe trousers pants and huge neat dreadlocks which were looked upon with disapproval among some in our very conservative neighborhood. His mother was English and his father was from the Caribbean, a relatively unusual background for those days. He inherited the good looks of both. He usually kept to himself on the bus. I was one of the few schoolboys he spoke to, one of the few who got beyond his seemingly intimidating manner and saw how nice he was.

Second Bus Stop—This stop was near the sweet shop; the last in a small parade of corner shops that sold all the daily requirements of the neighborhood—from greengrocer to butcher. Here the tall O'Brien brothers would get on. They might have been basketball stars if they were born in America. Tragedy would befall the family as the years wore on. The youngest boy died unexpectedly from a heart attack, and another son, Vince, died in a mountain climbing or hiking accident. Their Irish mother would appear early in the morning on our doorstep to ask my mother where her son was. John sometimes slept over after a night out with my brother Regi, usually drinking at a local pub or at a concert of the latest new music group. There were no cellphones in those days, and public red painted call boxes dotted around the area rarely worked or were occupied a good part of the day. Our phone box was often occupied by horse racing addicts, punters calling their bookies to check on winnings at Wincanton race track. We were one of the few houses that had a phone, a prized novelty worthy of idle bus stop chatter about the telephone pole wires going into number twenty-four.

Third Stop—Here the fiery O'Conner sisters would get on the bus. They lived in the upscale houses at the top of the hill on the road heading towards the charming and quintessentially English Mill Hill Village. The younger sister was of a rebellious nature and had lately turned into a punk rocker with Doc Marten's boots and spiky dyed red and blue hair. I believe she later became a doctor. Her elder sister seemed embarrassed by the showiness of her boisterous sister. I wondered what the very conservative and prudish nuns at St Michaels made of her.

I preferred the English sensibility of the Howard sisters. Us school children were mostly blissfully unaware of other passengers as we told jokes and teased each other. Occasionally an OAP (Old Age Pensioner), usually a Second or First World War veteran, annoyed that some kid or other did not offer him a seat would complain to the bus driver who would make an appropriate announcement over the bus loud speakers: "Get off them bloody seats! They are for OAPs not you kids." The threat of being thrown off the bus was usually enough to quiet our raucous crowd, even the English Smith brothers, the eldest of whom could be a handful if annoyed.

Several Bus Stops Later—As we neared the school, the Spanish Inquisition would board in the form of the inquisitive and jovial Blanche brothers from Madrid, Spain. The younger, very genial Carlos was in my class, and his two elder twin brothers were several years ahead of us. One twin was slim and the other was fat; they didn't look at all like brothers, let alone twins. They were mad motorcycle enthusiasts and Charlie (as we called Carlos) would end up with a leg in a cast after a dreadful smash-up. They were a gentle family. The father was either a banker or diplomat and they lived two towns over in the nicer section of old Hendon. Sometimes a curious friend of my elder brother would also board the bus here, a very exotic young man by the uncommon name of Hikko Flaherty. Hikko was half-Japanese and half-Irish. Such parental combinations at that time were simply unheard of. That was about as much as I knew about him. A cigarette smoking dandy with movie star looks, he was apparently famed among the girls at St. Michaels.

We piled off the bus just past the bridge where the tube train ran overhead from West Finchley to Woodside Park. We walked in small groups at various paces down a country alleyway that ran parallel to the train line, picking and eating ripe juicy blackberries in the brambles along the way. Twenty minutes later, frigidly cold and usually wet, we would enter the school's back gates by the caretaker's lodge, for a few minutes of playground banter and football (soccer) before the bell would ring for classes to start.

Scoundrels, Bonuses and Bounders

"The most important thing . . . is not winning but taking part." This is the Olympic ideal espoused by its founder, *Pierre de Coubertin*, which I've always thought defined the pinnacle of sporting excellence. Today winning is paramount even if it means cheating. Cheating in sports and many other pastimes seems near epidemic levels. Professional athletes routinely cheat in baseball, cricket, cycling, football, track and field and other professional sports. Athletes take drugs to enhance their performance and players throw cricket matches to benefit betting syndicates and to earn a payoff. The astronomic amount of money in sports today makes the stakes of winning incredibly high. Winning is everything for many and fair play counts for naught. College students are in on the act as well, cheating in exams even at some of the country's finest educational establishments. In business too, there is a desperate scramble to win. The names of Bernie Madoff in finance and Ben Johnson, and Lance Armstrong in sports, come immediately to mind.

The culture of high profile cheating in the world of business and finance seems to have gathered pace in the last decade judging by the quantum of recent fines. J.P. Morgan alone has been fined $20 billion for transgressions. Regulators appear hardly able to keep up. They are perpetually playing catch-up—outgunned, outmaneuvered and outsmarted by those they are charged with regulating. Spectacular multi-billion dollar fines are levied and paid without much fuss and the cycle of misdeeds continues unabated. The same tainted bankers remain on the job pretending the culture of their institution has reformed. Unlike the 1980s Savings and Loans crisis, nobody or, more precisely, very few, go to jail—it seems they all have the coveted *"Bankers' pass."* Those serving sentences like Madoff are relatively uncommon in an industry plagued with racketeers.

Alarming practices were rampant in the banking system, which caught regulators asleep at the wheel. In the recent financial crisis it was not uncommon to witness some of these spectacles in everyday matters of commerce. For example, I went to a real estate closing where the bank did not have the deed and title documents for the property on which it had given a mortgage. In short, the mortgage was written on a virtual property. The fantasy mortgage in turn had been sold on and repackaged as a financial mortgage security. Nobody seemed to care except for the stunned unfortunate couple buying the property. They of course sought the deed and title documents as proof of ownership for what they were paying for—since they had not bargained on owning a virtual multi-million dollar New York coop apartment. I even know of a major bank that routinely fabricated statements, just like Madoff. They did not have the actual securities that belonged to clients and were listed in the statements. When challenged, clients were told, "Oh, it's nothing to worry about. Just a *minor irregularity*, all will be resolved soon. Rest assured you won't lose a penny and, if you do, well, the bank will make it right." It is unclear whether regulators have now caught up with these fine institutions and whether any penalties have been imposed for this particularly sordid irregularity. I do know that customers are still waiting for their securities and dividends—although one would think if customer securities and dividends cannot be located, compensation should have been paid, as in the Madoff debacle, for their loss. It is too much I suppose to expect the kind of fairness espoused by *Pierre de Coubertin,* and to give customers their due—what is rightly theirs. One suspects that these were some of the *"socially useless,"* activities that Britain's Lord Turner was referring to when describing the deplorable state of today's banking and finance.

Few lessons seem to have been learned from the above crisis. This is epitomized in the continuing bonus culture in the finance industry. Wall Street's bonus culture remains an intriguing mystery to me. I am unclear why people should be paid a bonus even when the company they work for and are a part of is leaking—i.e., not making a profit. Does this imply that bonus recipients have contributed inordinately to the hole below the Plimsoll Line, making it smaller than it might otherwise have been? I don't know, but it seems absurd and nonsensical to me, and I suspect to many others outside of the confines of Wall Street.

Before the previous financial crisis—the so-called *dot com crisis*—around the turn of the century, I used to oversee what is called a country fund. I recruited a Wall Street professional to our team to help with arcane financial analytics. He was an MBA who unusually was both technically savvy and erudite. When it came to the bonus season he asked to speak to me about how much he might expect. I explained that in our august establishment bonuses were only paid if the firm made a profit. He seemed stunned at my immense ignorance, and said: "This is Wall Street; bonuses are paid irrespective of the bottom-line!" I repeated the firm's position as he walked away, presumably to dial his headhunters to request a better position with a rosy bonus outlook. It transpired that the *dot com* crisis soon set upon us, and our fund was tossed about in high seas. Like everyone else, we suffered heavy losses, and many sleepless nights trying to plot strategies to right our ship. All were in vain, since in market parlance, all markets had become positively correlated and followed one single rapid directional path—down! We worked late covering developments in Asian markets and came in early to monitor the fortunes of the markets in Europe.

One morning, walking down Park Avenue around 6:00 am towards our midtown offices, I encountered a phalanx of Frenchmen, as I was about to cross the road. One gentleman, the leader it seemed, placed his arm across my chest and swept me gently to the side so that his entourage could pass to the other side of the street. He had a relaxed, perhaps even regal air about him. I sensed tension among his disciples, some of who appeared to be sporting wires coming from their ears. For a millisecond I feared a sudden barrage of gunfire. But their tension eased as the tall gentleman bestowed a beatific smile upon me and pressed on up Park Avenue. When I arrived at the office I turned on the television for an update on global markets and was stunned to see a gentleman featured in the news report that looked remarkably like the man I had just encountered moments earlier on Park Avenue. It was, if my early morning eyes were not deceiving me, *Jacques Chirac*, the President of France from 1995 to 2007. He was attending the UN General Assembly.

It was a curious start to a day that would become more curious. I settled down to check our trading records since we were due to host one of the banks we traded with to reconcile activity, which had been particularly heavy during the crisis, as participants tried to outguess the market. Such operations, as a result, were necessary to align and offset trading positions. At this moment my new recruit came in and confessed. He had conducted losing unauthorized trades, which were about to be revealed with the reconciliation exercise. My recruit was a rogue trader! Not of the dizzy majestic—multi-billion US dollar scale—of rogue gallery legends: *Nick Lesson, Toshihide Iguchi, Yasuo Hamanaka, Jerome Kerviel,* and *Kweku Adoboli*. Nevertheless he had caused sufficient damage to mark the end of our growing niche fund. I wondered what could have motivated a smart individual from a prestigious business school to engage in such an unprofessional behavior. A coveted Wall Street bonus was the only conclusion I could come to. After that single incident, we disbanded our fund, which had otherwise produced spectacular returns and at one stage was the best performing fund in its category in the world.

I've long been a fan of the haberdashery, John Lewis, a quintessential English establishment where all the employees are partners and share equally in the firm's profits. Bonuses are paid only if the firm makes a profit. The firm is also renowned for its benevolence to all its employees and provides a range of extraordinary facilities for its partners. All partners can partake of these facilities and other benefits, from the lowest man or woman on the totem pole to the highest executive. There are no fiscally anointed *Prima Donnas*—blessed rock stars or rainmakers, as they are called on Wall Street. Independent innovation is rewarded with modest but meaningful perks and cash grants. This model has always struck me as perhaps the best to ensure a safe Wall Street that does not resemble an opium gambling den, filled with weapons of mass destruction. It is also apparently a winning formula that delivers year-after-year for its partners, i.e., without scandal or global destruction of the economies of the civilized world. Its partners live modestly but comfortably within the communities they serve—yes, serving, not exploiting or extorting.

Beyond banking, sports and colleges, the cheating culture has also spilled over into some of the most unlikely professions—e.g., architecture. I knew of a prominent architect with first class credentials who routinely pushed clients during the roaring decade in Manhattan to undertake ambitious projects she knew they could not complete. She would then sue them in cahoots with a relative who was a lawyer. I happened to bump into the architect's cousin in a bar by a random quark of fate, who told me quite openly about these shenanigans in animated detail. From all accounts it was a very successful and lucrative scam at the margins of the law. I received a frantic email from a respectable academic on sabbatical abroad, some months later, asking if I might share my own experience with the said architect. I had also been an unwitting victim of the charade. She was desperate to escape an out of control project and saw the writing on the wall as to how it would all end. She was trapped in a diabolical set-up. I've had the misfortune in recent years to have dealt with the vicissitudes of civil and commercial court system, so I could understand the academic's trepidation.

Winning at all costs, which some mistakenly believe is the *American Ideal*, remains paramount for far too many today—particularly for those scoundrels and bounders among us.

Gun Country

Having grown up in England at a time when police carried nothing but a wooden truncheon for protection, coming to America and seeing police with side arms took some getting used to. America's gun culture is complicated and difficult to comprehend until you go into communities where firearms are commonplace. As a Frenchman recently said in *The New York Times*, Americans are about as likely to give up guns as the French are to abandon their cradle-to-grave social welfare system.

The first time I came across a firearm firsthand was on a New York subway in the mid-1980s, when I was on the way home from work downtown on the Number One local. Some sinuous youths jostled onto the train, which was full of Wall Street bankers in expensive pinstripe suits, all very weary after a long workday. Subways back then were unreliable and graffiti covered. Doors were prone to open unexpectedly. Sometimes errant doors dumped unsuspecting passengers onto live rails and into the path of oncoming trains. Empty carriages as the train approached the crowded World Trade Center subway stop, usually meant a ride accompanied by the stench from a homeless person, with swollen appendages and alarming weeping sores, stung by your own guilt and helplessness at what you were witnessing, and no air conditioning. Tempers frayed. It was not unusual for shouting or pushing skirmishes to ensue, usually among the testosterone laden *Suits*.

On the day in question, the youths and the *Suits* shoved for space on the train and a few not so mild words were exchanged on both sides. This was the summer of 1986, and the trial of Bernard Goetz the infamous subway vigilante who shot several African-American youths, who tried to mug him, was nightly news. There was palpable tension in the air. Passengers including myself clung extra tightly to the glistening chrome hand rails in the car, buttocks clenched in preparation for flight at the next stop in case carnage broke out in the car. As the pile of *Suits* and youths jostled at one end of the carriage, a deranged homeless man proclaimed his own dramatic monologue: "I know what I am talking about. You're a simpleton brute! Stay away from my girl! I won't tell you again!" His ragged smelly presence at the far end of the carriage ensured that there was ample fuel for the fracas to spark. The rivals were full of manly pride until one of the red bandana clad youths lifted his plaid shirt to reveal a black magnum tucked neatly into his belt. All the passengers held their breath and the crowd of sweaty dripping *Suits* parted like Moses and the Red Sea.   The *Suits* pressed themselves and other passengers against the inside walls of the carriage in a desperate search for a means of escape. The young man's gold teeth glinted in the dimly lit subway as the train's wheels screeched and we pulled into the brightly lit Franklin Street Station. The youths, by now laughing at their own antics, jumped off the train. The collective pulse rate in the car dropped several hundred beats, and pounding hearts and clenched buttocks relaxed.

What I remember most vividly about the incident was the calm during the rest of the ride from Franklin Street to 79th, and the placid faces of my fellow riders. Some even returned to reading their mangled *Wall Street Journals* as if nothing of note had happened. I was shaken but now counted myself among the ranks of true battle-hardened New Yorkers.

My next firearm encounter was some years later in Naples, Florida, on a visit to the trailer park home of my girlfriend's parents. Her father was a retired Lieutenant Colonel from the United States Army and I had been forewarned that guns might be present in their home. I arranged accordingly for us to stay at the nearby Naples Hyatt not wishing to be the victim of an errant bullet from an alcohol loving military man who had only recently learned to appreciate individuals of color as fellow beings. We had a pleasant visit to their home with one major exception. Her grandmother took the occasion to bequeath her twelve-gauge shotgun to our little darling, presumably to ensure rapid attention at the crowded Fairways supermarket check-out on the Upper West Side. He was offended when I politely refused their offer and suggested they keep the thoughtful gift in Naples instead where our daughter might have a use for semiautomatic weapons. Guns were an engrained part of their family culture, a prerequisite to shooting and killing enemy combatants. One of my girlfriend's sisters and her husband were local law enforcement officers and apparently on occasion exchanged fire with undocumented, presumed criminal elements of the local Mexican population. This was all very unnerving for someone, like me, a former political exile, for whom firearms were an unwelcome reminder of civil conflict and violent death I had narrowly escaped.

More recently during a Spring Break trip to the home of one of my college roommate's in Parsons, Kansas, my family visited the farm next door to see their new-born calves. John's farmer neighbor, who bore a striking resemblance to Elmer Fudd, gave us a tour of his delightful grounds. He even let my six year-old son ride in his tractor. Then he proceeded to give us a brief tour of his home. From his living room we heard ruffling in the basement below. The sound was his son, a veteran of the Iraqi conflict who was suffering from post-traumatic stress syndrome. From what we gathered, he rarely ventured out of the dark confines of his below ground abode.

We were invited into the farmer's workshop, which was a veritable playground filled with all manner of mechanical contraptions: ploughs, motorcycles, water jets and more tractors of various sizes. He beckoned with a proud grin for me to come and see his giant double-door refrigerator-sized safe in a secured anteroom inside his workshop. The room was plastered with flaking posters of young thinly clad athletic women with radiant smiles and boobs to match. My immediate thought was that he wanted to show me piles of cash he used to pay his farm workers, which seemed strange but no stranger than some of the other things we had thus far witnessed. He carefully turned the combination of the dials on the Fort Knox like safe and gently swung open the heavy door to reveal an arsenal of weapons: rifles and guns of all shapes and sizes. He picked up a sharp shooter's rifle and smiled with a glint in his eyes as he gazed through the digital night vision telescopic sight. Then he lifted his golden prize, what seemed to me to be an AK-47—a *Kalashnikov* rifle. A former navy commando, he was adroit at handling each weapon in his arsenal. As I observed, I drew comfort in knowing that if Parsons were ever invaded, this farmer alone could withstand an assault from a battalion of soldiers for some considerable period—leaving ample time for the cavalry to arrive. The numerous "No Firearms Permitted Inside" signs we met with on bank, shop, restaurant, and church windows, indicated that Elmer Fudd would not be alone in the defense of Parsons. I left town no more informed than when we arrived about the connection between modern dairy farming, bovine birthing techniques and *Kalashnikovs*.

My gun country encounters taught me that while the Wild West is no more, the culture of guns lives on among some who still see owning firearms as a God given right—just like the French see their welfare state as inalienable. "I hunt therefore I am," is the maxim of many gun lovers, urban and otherwise. I will have to learn to get used to seeing weapons from time-to-time under unaccustomed circumstances.

Mental Health

Mental wellbeing is one of the most neglected parts of our lives. Living in New York where Woody Allen's neurotic characters portraits are famed, I have some understanding of the traumas that ill mental health can cause.

In New York there is a sizable community of private psychologists, psychiatrists and therapists who ply their trade in serene pastel painted rooms with leather chairs, helping sufferers find equilibrium and manage their lives. I would hazard a guess that rent, gym membership and therapy rank among the top ten expenses for many New Yorkers. In some New York circles, going to therapy is fashionable and *de riguer*, but for others the realities may be a little different.

Behind all this lurks the shame, stigma, fear and ignorance that sadly are associated with mental illness, even today. As a late uncle, who was a pioneering psychiatrist explained to me, we forget that not too long ago, the mentally ill were viewed as sorcerers and heretics. Not too long after that they were kept in deplorable conditions in asylums—subjected to depraved depths of inhumanity, medical and other unsavory forms of experimentation.

Interestingly, the World Health Organization (WHO) reports that there appears to be a high correlation between the wealth of nations and mental illness. In New York, this might be exacerbated by a lack of healthy daily social interaction and support. Despite the vast number of people in the city, many New Yorkers are lonely. They live behind anonymous bolted doors. Most barely know the names of their neighbors. Doorkeepers, elevator men and superintendents further reduce the need to interact with neighbors. At work social lines may be carefully managed so as not to reveal mental illness and to imperil prospects for career advancement. As a result, sufferers may feel further isolated. The social fabric of the City for the most part is devoid of interwoven multigenerational family ties one finds in urban communities like Mumbai, Beijing or indeed, Lagos, where tight knit communities support individuals, warts and all, through testing times. New York City today, is not a place where people know the problems that linger within each family.

One time, an individual came to my firm for an interview in the morning and we heard from the news that evening that he had stepped in front of a train and was killed instantly. Apparently, he had been job searching for months and was depressed although he showed no signs of this whatsoever at his interviews. The margin between healthy and not is often a very fine line that even professionals struggle to define.

The recent spate of gun violence against the general public provides, at the extreme, testimony to the dangers of neglected mental health care for patient and victims alike. Many people with mental health issues live good lives and learn to manage their illness with medication and therapy in the same way someone with diabetes or torn muscles might. Society as a whole however seems to attach an underserved stigma to mental health which makes those who may have a temporary bout of depression reluctant to seek help lest they be labeled as unstable or troubled. Education and changes in attitudes and perceptions are keenly needed. I had no appreciation myself for the breadth of people from all occupations and social class affected by depression and other related mental health issues until relatively recently when I witnessed the turmoil it can cause in my own household. A partner who is not well can soon dispel any thoughts that the illness is something others experience. It was sobering for me to see firsthand the bizarre narratives and sinister thoughts of even conspiracy that can be triggered by the illness.

We witness the signs daily among many of our peers but may not recognize them for what they are. Withdrawn or hyperactive in some cases, irritable, feeling disconnected from their bodies and their surroundings in others. Often not knowing or comprehending what the cloud is that suddenly drapes over them turning all to gloom.

Although controversy exists among researchers as to the effectiveness of pervasive drug treatment for mental health—the science of modern medicine is doing much to alleviate the *Blues* for many. But I can't help but wonder how much better it would be for those afflicted if they were able to more openly share their pain without being labeled as abnormal or weird. Normal, after all is a relative statistical term since we all come in many shapes, sizes, colors and with differing abilities and moods. A standard deviation from the "norm" in any of the above categories is hardly reason to shun large segments of our population. Mental wellbeing is an essential part of our lives and socialization. Mental health advocacy is important. Better understanding and education is dearly needed to provide a more positive face to mental illness—to show that it can be managed and overcome. I was encouraged on this front to hear that the Obama administration has now included mental health in its health care reforms with the goal of making care more readily available. A progressive and enlightened measure that is sure to save lives.

Finding True Love in New York

If you are looking for true love in New York, take the advice of its infamous "No Parking" signs. "Don't even think about it!" Your surest bet is to leave and to continue your search elsewhere far from the gaze of the Statue of Liberty, unless you are fortunate enough to stumble upon an unsuspecting tourist, preferably a first time visitor who is unfamiliar with the crazy tenets that drive romance in this magnificent urban jungle. The merest whiff of New York's alluring elixir means innocence is lost.

Romance in New York can be a brutal calculating affair. It can often resemble a mix between a keenly negotiated financial transaction and NATO military exercises. It may be advisable to bring your resume, physician and relevant good health certificates, credit score or private banker, lawyer with pre and post-nuptial agreements, therapist, allergist and dog-walker, to a first date. If you are a born and bred New Yorker, you have the distinct advantage of already knowing all of this beforehand.

Love, I've found, comes in many different varieties. As the Cole Porter and Ella Fitzgerald song goes:

I've been through the mill of love

Old love, new love

Every love but true love

The most popular flavors of love in New York City are: doomed, tragic, erotic, absurd, innocent, seductive, adulterous, and murderous. In New York, you must, in particular, learn to avoid the city's concentration of troubled souls whose veneer of normalcy conceals turmoil within. Regular New Yorkers know the types and are adept at recognizing and ducking them—those sullen with a faint medicated aura, overly charming and famously nice, kooky, wild, beautiful and erratic, all at once. These jumbled up, *femme and homme fatales*—with low activity in key parts of their frontal and temporal lobes—will leave you conned and emotionally bewildered.

Vigilance is of the utmost importance in dating in New York. Like the city's complex parking signs, New York has its own indecipherable dating codes. Don't take anything for granted, be proactive and informed about your prospective date lest you are taken in by a dastardly phony. Research and take references from friends and relatives if you can. It does not hurt either to know your zip codes since an Upper East Side investment banker may defer markedly in tastes, scruples and politics from a Hipster in hip Williamsburg, Brooklyn. Above all avoid spontaneity and impulsive behavior because these are the signs that the predators love. To sidestep unnecessary disappointment, remember not all are imbued with the same capacity for love that you have. There is nothing wrong in New York with approaching romance gingerly. In fact you may find it ultimately safer for your emotional wellbeing.

New Yorkers don't leave love to chance, they plan and research and position for maximum success. Competition is fierce particularly among the jaded over forties set—already cynical from failed multiple relationships. Dating for those with children is fraught with additional complications. These complications require even more vigilance, as Mia Farrow discovered with Woody Allen. In New York, you need uncommon sense to find love.

Interestingly the word love does not exist in Ibo, the language my parents spoke at home. Love in Ibo lexicon hovers between tenderness and respect. It is an ideal whose ponderous weight is firmly grounded in real life. This is in stark contrast to the Western love, as I discovered growing up in England and later America. Strong and unexplained emotional currents—deep inexplicable feelings, drive western love. It appears magical like a genie released from a mystical bottle. No straitjacket can contain this emotion. It is a passionate, reckless, uncontrolled love.

Love, attraction and romance, like the city's skyscrapers, assume new heights in New York—they lurk in the most unlikely places, e.g., the queue at *Citarella*, a popular fishmonger, the women's shoe department at Bloomingdales in Soho or while waiting for little Johnny or Miranda to emerge after dismissal from school. You need to be vigilant to tune into love in New York. To recognize the intricate mating calls of New Yorkers, like the ever so subtle brush of a shoulder or arm, or hello said at the salad bar with eyes briefly but firmly fixed on yours.

New Yorkers oddly are not like their counterparts in London or Paris who flirt constantly and feel quite safe in sharing their unequivocal interest. New Yorkers are more circumspect, with good cause. There are no rounds of boorish dinner parties here where guests are pre-vetted to ensure maximum compatibility. New York apartments with their nook-sized kitchens are simply too small for most to entertain. You generally have to find your own way in New York; aptly named blind dates are the closest analog to Paris and London's cozy dinner gatherings.

There is also the online world with its own rules of engagement to avoid axe murderers, sociopaths, serial con artists and potential rapists. The mendacious promise of a perfect match is rarely realized, in spite of mathematical algorithms replacing human choice and emotion.

For complicated tri-cultural individuals like me, New York offers an anonymous haven but a devilishly difficult place to find a partner since its rules of romantic engagement run counter to one's basic instincts. A belief in the goodness of those with whom you commune will not get you far in the New York dating scene. On the contrary, it will leave you vulnerable to human predators, if you are unfortunate to cross their path. For those like me, to be successful within this context, you must retrain your senses to dance to a different beat—the beat of money and success. New York likes winners. It is not sufficient in New York to be nice, a quality on its own that will take you far in London or Paris, but barely out of the blocks here in New York. First you must have a lot of cash and belongings. Next, it doesn't hurt to be famous. Looks, intelligence and charm may actually place a distant last.

It is also helpful to stay close to the line, meaning that you are recognizable as a familiar type to the average New Yorker. In New York, you will, with time begin to distinguish oligarch wives, from those of billionaire hedge fund managers and at the extreme, the spandex clad partners of owners of single gear racing bikes. These subtle skills will help you define what you are looking for, assuming that is, you have some sense of your own role in the city.

Being different may be helpful elsewhere but not here in New York. New Yorkers like to stay with familiar territory. Edgy terrain will not cut it for the average New Yorker; they have enough of that in their daily toil. If you are ready to play and live by its rules you will likely find success—what New Yorkers call "Real Love." If you want to keep your soul, again, look elsewhere for what the innocent, non-New Yorkers, call: "True Love."

Gym Membership

Gym going is nothing more than a simulated activity. It is not even half as good as the real thing. It is unnatural and carried out by those who do not know better.

While we walked through fields and talked on a warm summer's afternoon about life and the seasons, my friend Rachel shared with me her consternation at New Yorkers who spend endless hours exercising in air-conditioned gyms. She was tall and athletic with long strides; a basketball player in her youth. She said: "The spectacle of gym membership is enough to make you sick. Exercise should conjure up images of ancient Greek Olympians competing exposed to the elements. Athletes and exercise are like gladiators in mortal combat in the coliseum, not people clad in designer wear cowering indoors running on treadmills that rightly should be the exclusive preserve of hamsters," I couldn't agree more.

It has been a long time since I visited a gym. My memory of the last establishment I was in was of thinly clad men and women of various ages and shapes posturing like peacocks discussing the merits of detoxing, cores and body fat density. Meanwhile, others honed their bodies racing on stationary bicycles, treadmills and Stairmaster, pretending they were there solely for matters of health. With white towels over one shoulder and water bottles in-hand, gym members drifted from apparatus to apparatus in fashionable *sportif* attire stretching muscles and sinews—panting and puffing breathlessly. Chiseled athletic gym instructors passed on pithy directions to hapless members dripping with sweat. The place was filled with people to the gills, almost all sporting ubiquitous headphones connected to music playing devices. The smell of chlorine, testosterone and hints of pheromones filled the air. There were young men with chests protruding and biceps bulging. Ghastly middle-aged men with paunches held not so firmly in with darting eyes, receding hairlines and remaining strands of hair flicked deftly over bald patches. They lingered in the reception area, now showered and dressed in fancy pinstriped power suits denoting their eligibility for romantic dalliance or a second, third or fourth marriage. Young taut *Sex in the City* type women flaunted silky manes, overflowing bosoms and waxed legs. Their older middle-aged counterparts peddled furiously to restore youthful tone, while staring through the corners of their eyes at fit young male bodies in *situ* to blackout fuzzy unpleasant images of middle-aged husbands with flabby jowls. Thoughts of domestic life mingled with drifting fantasies.

Gyms are nothing but forums for social activity masquerading as emporiums for exercise. They sap dollars from those too feeble to realize that vigorous activity of many sorts is sufficient to provide the exercise they crave and all for free. This however does not include getting off the couch in the middle of the Super Bowl or the World Series to retrieve a beer from the refrigerator. Abandon your gym membership, and instead play soccer or Frisbee with your daughter or son in the park. Take up gardening, if you are fortunate enough to have a garden. Go hiking in the Hudson Valley with friends or simply ride a bike around town. Carry the groceries home rather than have them delivered and make sure you walk twenty blocks or more briskly each day. Take the stairs rather than the escalator where possible. Above all, make time for intimate exercise with your significant other since this also burns calories fast. You may also find it more pleasurable and scenic than riding a stationary bike. Most importantly eat well but sparingly and avoid junk food however enticing. Take up yoga in the morning. Karma is yours for the asking.

Only subscribe to gym membership if you are a professional athlete or your profession demands a perfectly sculpted body. If none of the above applies, skip the membership and try a dose of healthy clean living.

Single Dad—A Typical Kids Weekend

Friday Evening—"When are you coming home?" I normally receive a short text response within an hour or so from my daughter, indicating her ETA. Sometimes when more complicated arrangements are on the cards for the weekend, then I might receive a phone call usually to say that she has a school event or a sleepover with one of her classmates. I start winding down my day in readiness to leave the apartment to pick up my son from after school chess club at 5:00 pm. By 4:45, I am dashing out only to be delayed by the pre-war elevator, which takes an eternity to arrive ominously on my floor, the thirteenth floor. I fear being accosted by a chatty neighbor in the elevator who will no doubt make me late or think me rude in my unexplained haste. Lateness usually means a sober lecture on punctuality from my seven-year-old.

I dash out of the building with no sense of the weather. My days are compressed; mornings are spent dealing with European clients over the phone. I make it just in time to collect my son among the sea of parents and children milling around the hallway in the school entrance. My son tells me about his latest nifty chess moves. These moves have worked magic and produced several victories against more accomplished adversaries. He is proud and pleased to share his news with me. We detour en route home for glazed donuts to celebrate his chess accomplishments. Dunkin' Donuts, is a vibrant after school hub, it's teeming with children and caregivers negotiating which donuts to buy.

By the time we are at the apartment, my daughter's text arrives informing me she will not be home until 9:30, which means she will miss dinner. Dinner together is a key event in our household, so my son and I are naturally disappointed. I ponder whether to enquire further why she will be so late and decide to leave that question until she is actually here. Post-donut snack prepared, Digestive Biscuits and smoked salmon, a favorite, my son settles to watch his most favored cartoons, his end of week treat. I return to my home office to clear my desk and jot down any writing thoughts. We reunite to prepare dinner together in our bi-weekly ritual with the BBC World Service serving as a background for our father and son conversations. These conversations run the gamut of subjects that intrigue inquisitive 7 year-old minds. Christmas is approaching and the latest I've been asked is "Why is Jesus so famous?" I am still working on an answer that will be satisfactory in its sufficiency. The conversation moves to the children's book he has asked me to write for him. He tells me it has to be a series and must have characters on adventures. We pick amusing names that would resonate with 7 year-olds for the two main characters. Dinner done, bath time follows. Then story time—*Babar Comes to America*, by Laurent de Brunhoff and *The Enormous Crocodile*, by Roald Dahl, for the umpteenth time. I can't say no. My son never wearies of the same story, even if I have. I struggle to keep my eyes open and soon my son is asleep and so am I. In between, my daughter has arrived and is ensconced in her room with door closed. I wake up after my brief snooze, and check on her. "How was school?" I ask and, "Where did you go afterwards?" "Another college recruiting event," she says, "McGill University from Canada." "A great school," I say. But I wonder how I would survive frigid parents' weekends in Montreal. It's a cultured city which I happen to like very much in the spring or summer. "I got an A in my 'Org' mid-term," she says smiling proudly. I ask, thinking myself amazingly clever, "is that organic chemistry?" She nods yes with an expression that says she knows I'm clueless what that means, and retreats happily back to her room. Now alone in the sitting room after 10:00 pm, I exhale and reflect on my day. Red wine filled to the circular dual-band of the shallow conical *Duralex* glass, I wallow in the resounding joy seeing my daughter and son brings. This is the tragic dilemma of the father who because of separation from their mother, only sees his children bi-weekly with a mid-week dinner in-between.

Saturday—Unlike his teenage sister, my son is an early riser. He is up even before dad, playing his music, usually *Adele*, perched on his bed reading books. Next he keeps busy building amazing flying Lego fantasies. As 9:00 am approaches, like clockwork, he is in my room announcing: politely "time for my Frosted Flakes." I lie in bed momentarily hoping I've remembered to restock, otherwise he will have to make do with Cheerios. First part of breakfast completed. Showers taken, faces washed, teeth brushed and hair combed. Now time to pick up the papers at the corner shop. There the line is long with those struggling to keep body and soul together as they dictate lottery numbers to the pretty wife of the Indian proprietor who sits passive and attentive, listening from behind the counter. A Hindi soap opera blares from the TV behind her. Ten, seven, double zero and six, are carefully read out from a tattered piece of paper by a worn looking Latin lady with curlers in her hair, slippers and a headscarf.

Weekend FT (*Financial Times*) and *The New York Times* in our hands we drop our $5 on the counter, bypassing the growing queue of lottery punters and head for the door. There is a peculiar air about the gamblers, all seem to know their odds are slim but still play for the mere hope that playing brings. It's like a cheap legal fix—a shot of dopamine to the brain. New York's cool breeze meets our faces as the door opens and the lap dogs tied to a post outside let out yapping barks. Soon in the building foyer, we exchange morning pleasantries with the two cheerful doormen. "Nice day out there," "Yes it is," I reply as we make our way back up the groaning dawdling elevator to the apartment.

We make eggs, toast, juice and tea and have an animated discussion about whatever is on my son's mind. Today, it's the efficacy of Black Holes, and the relative speed of light around them. I listen eagerly and learn. Lecture over, father and son squeeze together into one of the comfortable side chairs and switch on the TV to watch our soccer game. My son reminds me not to fall asleep. He wants to watch his team, Manchester United and I want to watch mine, Tottenham Hotspurs. We settle on United.

Single Dad—A Typical Kids Weekend

I attempt to read some of the very interesting stories in the FT Life & Arts section before we venture across the park on foot to the Metropolitan Museum. My son wants to show me the medieval armor collection and other artifacts he thinks might be of interest to me. Knowing I have a passion for contemporary African Art, he also suggests that we explore that wing of the Met as well. Meanwhile, my daughter is up. Clues include the missing plate which has now presumably vanished to her room with breakfast on it. Sometime later before we depart, showered and dressed, she emerges and announces she is off for her sleepover. We will see her at noon the next day. She has a collaborative school project, she explains and her best friend has the relevant software at home on her parent's computer. We return in the evening after our fun outing to the Met with a sketch book for my son, who enjoys arts and crafts. He has already opened the package and is busy doing experimental doodling of geometric shapes. I've been talked into helping construct three dimensional cubes and exploring the shading of same.

Sunday—A haircut at the neighborhood barber where Jose will cut both our curls. The small waiting area is full this morning with a variety of Upper West Side types, a suited banker, and a mother with two children, a middle age Latin gentleman and a fashionable young African-American man dressed in low hugging jeans. The Jewish lady in between speaking Hebrew with her two kids passes instructions in fluent Spanish to one of the barbers who responds in kind and prepares to start styling the first child's hair. Jose is finally free and quickly gives me my usual ten minute short-back-and-sides. A slightly more nuanced haircut is in store for my son who has been busying himself playing magnetic darts with another waiting kid of about the same age. Our grooming complete, we collect his scooter and head for home.

Daughter is home when we arrive, visibly tired, not having slept much at her friend's. No doubt up late working as they cranked on their project, I hope. "How is Helen?" I ask calmly, "And her parents?" "Fine!" comes the reply, as she vanishes back into the cocoon of her room. Helmets secured, we are off with our bikes to the park. I hope this time round my son will remember to give adequate space to joggers, particularly those of the older variety, in the jogging lane, and Japanese tourists navigating crosswalks near Strawberry Fields. He felled an unfortunate jogger that stepped into the bike lane some weeks earlier as we hurtled downhill. No lawsuits on either side. Mercifully, save for a few tears from both, no one was physically hurt.

On our return, we order pizza—children's caviar—and commune once again around the dinner table. Brother and sister joking and teasing and me, daddy, running back and forth to the kitchen for dessert. Time now for drop-off at their mother's a short taxi ride away. Loving hugs are dispensed and wishes for a good week ahead. The end of another joyful weekend, I now have a sad two weeks ahead. The apartment will seem hollow and empty without their presence and their cheery voices, which takes over every nook and cranny when they are there.

I linger in the hallway of their building located in the newly vibrant and resurgent Harlem, and observe as a doorman greets every resident by name and residents in turn greet each other in like respectful manner. Brief tales are exchanged about the Knicks basketball game the night before or services for a neighbor who's passed away. Life flickers from monochrome to Technicolor. The elevator door closes, I wave goodbye and I step out into the cold evening air to head home on the No. 2 subway.

Harvard Reunion

College reunions are strange affairs; I had no understanding of their significance until I came to America to attend a college whose name when dropped at dinner parties, often causes a pause in conversation, as the "H-Bomb," sinks in. Harvard reunions are extraordinarily well planned affairs. Pre-reunion events occur months in advance in major cities around the world. Class members play a strategic role in the organization, planning and hosting of the events. They decide on their nature and also orchestrate fund raising. This, aside from promoting institutional loyalty, is the key objective of the reunion exercise. It is also a remarkable exercise in legacy. Alumni discuss their progeny; those already at Harvard and others who will be seeking to enter its esteemed doors.

Classmates gather for a long weekend of reconnecting, sharing and communing. I was recently at my 30th reunion, which provided sufficient time for most to have abandoned superficial airs and competitive streaks that blocked meaningful exchange. We all now have abundant experience to look back on, some rewarding, others not so much. Stars within the class, like Melissa Block, veteran NPR host and journalist, were integrated in the proceedings—in Melissa's case she was assigned to interview the college president, Drew Faust, in a town hall event. President Faust answered questions from alumni and talked eloquently about the future she sees for the institution and its energetic students. She stresses the choices the students are now making, to my delight, into more meaningful careers away from the financial world. College, she says, provides an opportunity to explore in a way many may never do again. A view I unequivocally share. Harvard's lifelong impact on our lives is disproportionate when measured next to our four-year experience on campus.

Success can come at a price. Life, you notice has clearly taken a toll on some classmates who look decidedly weather worn. There's some debate if this is correlated to their career paths—e.g., investment banking types mostly look prematurely gray and overweight, probably as a result of a public beating after the 2008 financial crisis. That's one of the biggest surprises at reunion, when someone greets you that looks like the merest shadow of who they were as you remembered them thirty odd years ago. Some wear the sorrows or happiness of their lives around their faces and bodies like a coat, sparkling or soiled, tattered and frayed. Either way, all seem illuminated and energized by being in each other's mostly safe company.

Old clusters of friends and rooming groups gather once again and float together around events. Delayed or new found romances blossom while others continue with the same failed destructive cycles that didn't work at college or at past reunions. Some still carry torches for classmates but with wives, husband and children in tow, reconcile that their paths are now fixed. They must find another way to ease their domestic misery. Some happy couples, college sweethearts, dot the reunion landscape and serve to give hope to those searching anew.

Other issues surface too, particularly those of success or lack thereof. For some, those who measure life by counting numbers—it is a major mark of achievement that they have made money and deem themselves, perhaps therefore, more important in life. The university certainly believes them of high import since it values their oversized giving perhaps unduly when measured against those of stars in other less remunerated, but no less important, professions—like, medical research of obscure genetic diseases. The latter in all likelihood, however, contribute disproportionately more in donations relative to their incomes. This said, there is a genuine leveling at reunion, people focus on who they are inside rather than their outside personas. Reunion celebrates the achievements of almost all classmates and serves as a forum for those who wish to showcase what they've done in the intervening thirty years. Most leave feeling good about how they've turned out and their achievements even if they fall short of changing the world. A minority, the overachievers, may leave feeling under achieved. But these are types that will always feel that way.

The preponderance of medical talent at these events means you needn't worry about sudden illness, a heart attack perhaps or a stroke. I was at one such event when the child of a friend fell and broke her arm. She was instantly attended by a phalanx of some of the best medical experts in the country. Similarly at our 30th, a popular and dear classmate had heart palpitations and had to spend the night hospitalized but from all accounts received expert care and attention from qualified classmates in his vicinity.

Networking is less of a feature of the 30th reunion, since most are now at the pinnacle of their careers or well in the midst of a mid-life crisis, i.e., reassessing, where they belong in life and in Harvard's illustrious community.

Perhaps the most moving event of the reunion is the service dedicated to those who have passed away, a grim reminder of your own mortality and how lucky you are to be alive. The sorrow for those lost classmates reverberates through Harvard's chapel. Tears are shed and hugs exchanged to console those swept away with grief in the somberness and poignancy of the moment. Psalms are recited and songs are sung in remembrance. The numbers of those who have passed away is likely to accelerate in the years ahead as we all battle the inevitable march of time. Some of the reunion lectures given by learned TED professor peers, echo this theme. The talks give a sense of the gap between *thinkers* and *doers* in our class. It seems clear that quality as well as quantity of life is on the minds of many for the next quarter century. The social richness of the event is diminished only by the lack of time to dwell and linger with so many amazingly wonderful human beings.

Saying Goodbye

"Gus, I'm dying,"

I heard the words on the telephone but they seemed incomprehensible. How could Nancy be dying? She was only 57 years old. I knew she had been unwell but such a rapid decline seemed implausible. She was Superwoman, who juggled a husband, two daughters and a demanding career. "Would you like me to come to visit, Nancy," I said. She responded, "Yes," in a weak rasping almost inaudible voice. There was gladness and I thought a glimmer of hope in her tone. "Is it okay if I come next week?" "Yes," she said adding quickly, "come!" we both hung-up.

I had no sense of the extreme urgency of her race between life and death, and that Nancy's time was as near as it was. The softness of her voice still echoes in my mind. This was the last time I spoke to Nancy; she was in her country home in Rhinebeck, New York, which she loved. I had bumped into Nancy some month's before in mid-town early one morning on the way to work. Her office was around the corner from mine but strangely we had hardly seen each other, not even for lunch. She didn't seem quite her usual confident effervescent self. I said I would drop by their mid-town apartment soon with the family. But my words did not seem to register as she made her way down Third Avenue. She casually waved a fainthearted goodbye. Nancy, a famed extrovert seemed unusually preoccupied with her own thoughts. I thought perhaps she was upset at me because I had missed her wedding. It was her second wedding. My college roommate and I had remained close with her first husband, David. We adored them both. I could not bring myself to go, since I was in the throes of my own domestic dramas and the wedding I recall was ominously on a bitter cold New York day with heavy snow.

I woke early one morning, several days after the call and retrieved *The New York Times* from my front door. It was a bright

Saying Goodbye

October morning and the light stunned me when I opened the living room blinds. Cup of tea in hand, I sat on the couch casually thumbing through the sports and business sections before leaving for work. I inadvertently stumbled on the obituaries, a section I rarely read. Nancy's name caught my eye as I turned the page. There to my shock was her obituary; I read the words slowly and deliberately to be sure. It said she had succumbed to "complications of amyotrophic lateral sclerosis (ALS), commonly known as Lou Gehrig's disease..." The words were heavy on me. Alone in my apartment, I sat still on my couch and quietly wept. Nancy was gone, I'd missed my opportunity to say goodbye.

I never saw Nancy with the ravages of ALS and can't help wonder if she wanted those close to her to remember her as she was —a beautiful scholar, mother, executive and a vivacious and thoroughly modern woman. The disease, from what I understood, was not kind in its savagery. I can only imagine how difficult it must have been for her daughter Courtney to cope with seeing her mother who loved life so much pass away.

Nancy was one of the most energetic and dynamic women I have ever known. She and her first husband, David, an equally extraordinary person, had been host family to my college roommate through our four years at Harvard. Beautiful, young and worldly, they were our surrogate parents and we shared many joys and pains of college with them. We had shared many fond memories together in their lovely home in Dorchester in Boston, Massachusetts. There was the annual ritual of *Pina Coladas* on their porch while we watched the US Open Tennis Championship and many parties at their home for various foreign dignitaries. They also hosted both our parents for graduation.

A perfect family, it appeared from our young eyes, we were very saddened when David and Nancy divorced but kept in close contact with each of them. They were both very special as were their daughters Courtney and Lindsey who we saw grow up into young remarkable women. Lindsey—whose soul was as beautiful as her face, tragically, a few years later died while giving birth to a handsome young son, the same age as my own. David and Nancy both independently visited Nigeria for work, and each made sure to visit with my father while they were there. Nancy was particularly fond of my outspoken, larger than life and self-possessed half-sister Lauretta, in whom I suspect she saw her own tall elegant confident self.

Just after Christmas this year, eleven years on from Nancy's death, my family was at Courtney and her husband's brownstone in Brooklyn with their two adorable children and lots of other guests. David was there with his charming and beautiful new wife Sarah. Sarah and I chatted about how I had mistakenly gone to JFK airport for our budget flight to Washington for their wedding, only to discover the flight was actually out of Newark. I had to scramble to purchase a new set of pricey last minute tickets for a rush flight from LaGuardia airport. It was probably, all told, one of the most expense roundtrips to Washington on record. I was not popular with my other-half that day but we did happily make it in time for their wonderful wedding. As they do every year, she and David had flown in from Portland where they retired, for the holiday event. It all seemed right as we celebrated together keeping our memories of Nancy and Lindsey to ourselves.

I couldn't recall the last time I had wept. It was probably as a child when we were fleeing probable death in Nigeria's bloody civil war. The next time after that would be when I received the news of my father's unexpected death early one morning two days before Christmas. It was a massive stroke. He died instantly at the wheel of his Volvo while parking in front of his sister's house. The fact that it happened so far away in Nigeria made the pain even more acute. Christmas has not had the same meaning for me since then. There was no goodbye; just numbness, profound shock and tears. The

Saying Goodbye

finality was incomprehensible at first. It was a new type of grief the depth of which I had never known before and that only those that have lost a parent, child or sibling can understand.

I remember accompanying my only aunt here in America to the Memorial Sloan-Kettering Cancer Center, which was around the corner from my office, regularly for radiation and chemotherapy treatment. I was sitting with her in the hospital the day the young baby-faced doctor told us that all was lost. Other desperate somber families sat in the waiting room and the gentle kind staff came in and out. The cancer was back with a vengeance, she had only days left to live. Aunt Franca, a religious woman, took the news stoically. A slender uncomplicated woman who was a beauty in her youth, she had once told me Central Park seemed such a waste when people were so crowded on Manhattan. She came to New York in the sixties and was jilted by her fiancée. She wanted to die in Nigeria, after living all her adult life in New York. My daughter accompanied me as we took her to the airport for the last time. My daughter was carsick and threw-up in the taxi as we arrived at JFK. I expected the cab driver to explode with rage, but instead he showed nothing but kindness, helping to clean up and assisting my aunt onto the sidewalk. It was as if he understood the real life story that was unfolding before his eyes. Perhaps he had seen this before in his cab. She was frail but still able to walk with her cane. She waved with resignation as we embraced and said goodbye at the departure gate; she slid into the British Airways wheel chair to head to passport control and the security x-ray machine to board the plane for her last flight. At the other end her favorite niece, also named Franca, would care for her. Several days later my cell phone vibrated and rang with an urgency that seemed more than usual. It was the younger Franca, who handed the phone to aunt Franca who gasped as she struggled to fill her lungs with air. I told her goodbye not sure she could hear me. The following day an early morning text announced her death.

I was glad we were able to say goodbye, it made the enormity of the grief and sadness somehow more bearable.

An American Tragedy

Some years ago a friend was making a documentary about a homeless family in New York. Over the next decade, I met and heard about the people magnificently chronicled in the groundbreaking documentary, including the mother and daughter after whom the film is titled.

The story of Hope and Craig is an American tragedy that's as poignant as Shakespeare's Troilus and Cressida. Young and in love they have four children and live in a rundown neighborhood of Brooklyn, New York, in an equally disheveled apartment. This however is no ordinary family. Both have AIDS, Craig knowingly having contracted it from Hope in what can only be described as a suicidal love pact. Issues of self-worth and hopelessness are spectacularly at play and Craig has knowingly played Russian roulette with his own life.

Their lives seemed doomed from the start. Both are from poor dysfunctional families where drugs and abuse were staples. They've struggled against all odds but have failed to break the cycle of dependence in a world where crack cocaine is rampant and teenage pregnancy is the norm. Children are one of the few forms of self-worth and expression that girls in the neighborhood have. An inadequate welfare state that's ill equipped for the damage and trauma their family has suffered has equally struggled to keep pace with their many real life calamities. The same mistakes keep repeating from generation to generation like an interminable curse. This unfortunately is the curse that so many economically and educationally disadvantaged African-American and other minority inner city youth face—how to survive and how to escape the viciously cruel Dickensian cycle of one-way tickets.

Their lives now hang in the balance and the fate of their four children ranging in age from six to sixteen remains unclear. In all likelihood they will be left without parents. Parents who themselves are still to reach the age of thirty. Hope's mother, Susan, is the poster child of the family. She survived crack addiction and deplorable shelter living with her children to gain her GED (General Education Diploma). She later found a respectable office job in the City. Having struggled so hard, we can only imagine the terrible pain Susan must be going through. She made it out, but her daughter and her family were pulled back in under the waves of perilous vicissitudes. She now faces the sorrowful prospects of being predeceased by her daughter. Hope, born with AIDS, faced dreadful odds for survival. Her children gave her hope and she helped them through the early drug regime that ensured that they too did not contract HIV.

This story is not a simple narrative; it is an American story that is not often told. It is the story of lives watched from afar through the prism of hope that they would pull through and defy the odds that were so very clearly stacked against them. And in so doing, somehow find redemption and their *American Dream*. It is hard now to watch and to accept as Hope and Craig's lives unravel and wash away. Despite good intentions, all around them have failed to reverse the cycle of early death in modern Hobbesian lives played out in callous urban surroundings. The question now is what can be done for their children to tip the balances for them. So much of our development and success in life is dependent on our formative years and the nurturing we receive. These children save for the eldest, have had only the merest glimmer of what they should have had and deserve. The many serious challenges in mental and physical development that lay ahead are well documented. They will likely face curtailed educational success which may portend failed lives once more. Much sadness, anxiety, self-loathing and shame may befall these children however resilient they are, if significant help is not at hand. They will have an additional social barrier to overcome when compared to their peers and will need exceptional luck, drive and grit to escape the gravitational pull that threatens to keep their orbit fixed around poverty and early death.

Hope and Craig are the forgotten face of America, the face that pricks our conscience and that many Americans neither understand nor want to see or hear about. The help of well-meaning citizens—do-gooders—has not been sufficient to alter the powerful downward force of a society that does far too little to help those at the margins—desperately in need from birth. Their probable premature deaths will be a failure not just for them and their families but for us as a society and the system as a whole. Hope has been carrying a burden all of her life—a death sentence.

Entrepreneurship

"I like the process of having an idea and then turning it into reality," the highly successful English men's fashion designer, Paul Smith once proclaimed. If you value your sanity, resist this impulse with all the might you possess, because for every Paul Smith, there are tens of thousands, if not millions, of abject and bitter entrepreneurial failures. Successful entrepreneurs, like Paul Smith, titter not so happily near the brink of the abyss before encountering success—often after many long years in the wilderness swimming against the tide driven by a singular belief in their enterprise. Entrepreneurship is as much about finding and testing your breaking-point as it is about making money. As a result, the constant companion of an entrepreneur is worry.

Being an entrepreneur is like running a marathon alone urged on only by the cheering crowd in your head—your ego and pride—it can result in what experts call "a delusionary sense of self." Arthur Conan Doyle, in describing forlorn 1908 Olympic marathon runner *Dorando Pietri*, who was disqualified for being aided by umpires after falling four times near the finish line to the grueling and ultimately heartbreaking 26.2 miles course, said: "It is horrible, and yet fascinating, this struggle between a set purpose and an utterly exhausted frame." *Dorando Pietri* lost the prize to second place American runner Johnny Hayes, but in the same instant became immortalized in the eyes of the sporting public. Watching an entrepreneur suffer can elicit similar pain and compassion, but rarely is there the altruistic desire to aid them over the line without extracting handsome compensation, even the gold medal. Finding backers can become a full-time preoccupation, which may make you more accustomed to the word "No" than you might like.

Entrepreneurs are optimistic by nature and are confident in their own abilities. They rarely factor in the importance of competition, luck and unexpected surprises on the outcome of their endeavors. These very traits will be precisely why some succeed—

the conviction to buck accepted convention and an unwavering belief in the correctness of their own hunches and rare ability. Nevertheless, remember you may heroically build a highway through impenetrable jungle overcoming imponderable obstacles, but it does not mean that motorists will actually want to use your monumental accomplishment sitting there in the midst of the plain.

For those of you with romantic notions of entrepreneurship and visions of mega billionaire Sir Richard Branson on his yacht moored off his Caribbean Island of Necker, let me tell you, this is actually an extremely hazardous, and mostly unglamorous profession. I would not recommend it for anyone who is feint of heart. Simply put, an entrepreneur is basically someone willing to shoulder years of hard work, with little or no pay, significant risk and more than likely utter financial ruin. Get ready to say goodbye to some close friends and more likely than not, your partner in life. Don't get too attached to anything of value because you are more than likely to lose it.

You will have to deal with the cunning of your customers and employees alike; the former, particularly if they are big organizations with their own complex internal culture and raging internecine battles. Egos will frustrate you and try to wear you down, perhaps even distract you from the task at hand, especially if your labors mean that they in turn now have to break a sweat at work.

Reward for entrepreneurs is a relative term. In all probability it will be psychic rather than fiscal. Your persistence and obstinacy may only prolong and balloon the cost of eventual failure. Double down and not up and then look in the mirror for sober crystal clarity. Entrepreneurs have less control on eventual outcomes than they actually realize. They too are susceptible to the random vagaries of life, even if they believe otherwise.

From a lifestyle perspective, as an entrepreneur, you will have the benefit sometimes of being able to choose who you work with, how and when you work. A balance of money and quality of life is the ultimate goal, but neither may come at the same time, leaving you, as per above, perilously close to ruin.

And finally, don't expect to be ringing the closing bell at the New York Stock Exchange anytime soon dressed in your Mark Zuckerberg lookalike hoody or any other apparel reserved for those on the winners' podium unless you are ready to look failure in the eyes multiple times.

Spooks on the Line

It was the mid-90s. I picked up the receiver and began to dial my European client's phone number on the rotary dial of my home office telephone. I waited for the phone to ring at the other end. As I waited, the rustling of papers on the line inadvertently interrupted my call. A stranger's voice interjected.

"Hello, hello..." the voice said softly, as if making sure there was nobody there before beginning his day's work.

The voice, realizing that the game was up and that they had been caught red-handed eavesdropping on my phone line, apologized hastily and hung-up. My phone was bugged. I had suspected as much, from the strange noises I heard periodically on the line. Sometimes it would be the bored sounds of a third party breathing or yawning rather heavily on the line. I always stopped short of asking, "Who is that," for fear I might be paranoid. Now my fears were confirmed for sure. It was like a scene out of a Cold War spy novel.

It was unclear why someone would bug my phone but I surmised that the eavesdropper was an aggressive business competitor. I had my suspicions about one in particular who had taken great pleasure in quoting back to me a sentence from a private phone conversation I had had with a corporate client that we were both in pursuit of for lucrative debt advisory business. I had mildly disparaged his firm and he was not pleased. This was the first of several strange phone incidents I would encounter in my years in New York.

The second incident was an unexpected evening call from an agent of the State. I was sitting in my midtown bachelor pad deep in my own thoughts, reading *Love in the Time of Cholera* by Gabriel García Márquez, when suddenly the phone rang. It was my home office phone which rarely rang after 7:00 p.m., so I was hesitant at first to answer. But eventually I walked down my narrow hallway to my office to silence the annoying din. When I picked up the receiver, I encountered a deep firm baritone voice on the other end of the line:

"Are you Augustine Udo?" he asked.

"Yes," I replied.

"I'm agent Jones from the Secret Service," he said calmly. I did not know at the time but it is apparently the job of the Secret Service not only to guard the President of the United States, but also to ensure the security of the nation's financial and payment systems.

"Is this a joke? If this is a prank, it's not at all funny to me!" I replied.

I dropped the receiver, thinking it was a prank call. Just like in the movies, the telephone immediately rang again.

"Mr. Udo, Do not drop the receiver again," responded the same voice, this time stern and annoyed.

"This is agent Jones from the Secret Service; did you make a wire transfer to Nigeria?"

"Yes," I answered.

"You made the wire from the National Westminster Bank."

"Yes."

"Your wire transfer was intercepted, but don't worry we have your funds and it will get to its destination."

Agent Jones then asked, "Why were you wiring money to yourself in Nigeria?"

I explained that the money was for my retired father after whom I was named. He is also called Augustine, like my grandfather before him, but with different initials. Like many immigrants, I sent regular wire transfers home to help family, this was not a surprising revelation worthy of the attention of the Secret Service.

"Okay, well that explains it. No need to do anything else, everything has been taken care of. Have a good evening!" He hung up.

I sat down in shock. Why would they have been eavesdropping on my line, I asked myself? Do they think I am some kind of crazy arms dealer? How many other calls were being monitored and wires intercepted? My life mercifully is not that interesting and must have been excruciatingly tedious for the poor sap assigned to my phone.

I chuckle respectfully when I hear about the current Edward Snowden *WikiLeaks* furor surrounding phone surveillance by the National Security Agency (NSA). As so many decry the sudden intrusion on our freedoms, some of us, foreign types, have to chuckle. Such intrusions have been the norm for us for years. We have long regarded intrusion as a price of our American freedom. It seems with the bounties of new ever more invasive technical prowess; the NSA's spymasters now have the ability to spread their tentacles into the business of all and sundry in a way that has hitherto not been possible. No longer is snooping targeted to a lucky few, vast electronic surveillance of phone, email and web browsing records, including it would appear, those of some of the leaders of the Free World—our allies no less—seems to be the order of the day.

Such amazing technological prowess makes the presence of an uninvited voice on my private phone line seem refreshingly quaint.

Promises—A Weekend in the Country

The summer was full of promise. On the rebound from a steady three-year relationship, I was in search of love. Instead I encountered Rachel, an attractive introspective divorcee who lived in a contemporary *Architectural Digest* home in a barn in upstate New York. We met at a college reunion event. We knew each other only slightly since we moved in separate circles. Rachel recognized me from across the room and waved to catch my attention. She mouthed "Gus," and motioned for me and my friend Tim to leave with her for a drink after the event. Rachel was a picture of desire. I was seduced by her charm. We soon started dating.

It was the start of an intense and electrifying summer. I became a weekend commuter like other Manhattan refugees on the Metro-North Hudson Line. A smiling Rachel awaited me at the other end of the line with her shining BMW chariot. Rachel had a muchness that included a wild heaped raven colored mane, radiant smile and a statuesque athletic figure. Perched on top of her tall frame was an agile mind full of curious debate. She was a wonderful cook and a molecular gastronome. For reasons that were unclear to me, she chose me as her muse for the summer. She seemed emotionally pained, inconvenienced even, when we were apart, which was more frequent than either of us would have liked. We were trying to work out our routine—I had my parenting responsibilities with my children who came to stay every second weekend and Rachel the daily upkeep of her farm property, corgi dogs, and a son in college. On weekends when we were together, Rachel could be found pottering—pruning, weeding shrubs, and trimming flowers. Her dexterous oversized hands gathered soil beneath nails. But unbeknownst to me, her confident tanned face and almost meditative manner bellied a stupefying character within.

I failed to comprehend Rachel, starting from the first night at her barn. It was—a star filled evening and we were outside grilling steaks on a bonfire when my cellphone rang. It was my college friend Rick who also happened to be acquainted with Rachel but did not know we had started seeing each other. Rick wanted to invite me to an event in Connecticut with his girlfriend, which was clearly not doable given my location, which I imparted, to Rick. I then handed the phone to Rachel. She chatted briefly with Rick and conveyed a false air of pleasant surprise at hearing his voice. Rick had not been too enthused at the prospect of me dating her, when we had discussed this earlier. He was frankly somewhat incredulous on the phone since he had signaled our incompatibility and I had obviously ignored him. To my folly, I elected, as I am apt to do with most people, to take Rachel at face value—I don't judge. Rachel handed back my phone saying goodbye to Rick with patronizing affection. Rick had now hung-up. As the stars twinkled and flames licked the embers from the burning crackling logs, Rachel asked rhetorically, "so you and Rick are very close friends?" As if to say this may be awkward down the line. It was a vivid moment which I recorded for future exploration.

We were now shucking corn for the grill, Rachel said she was going for a dip in the pool and I should join her once I had refilled our wine glasses in the barn. I returned to find Rachel with her back to me in the pool in the evening darkness with the soft pool lighting reflecting off the water on her tanned naked form. We were soon locked in amorous embraces but the promise of pleasure was short-lived, as Rachel wistfully announced, "It's too early for us to go further." I would discover over time that she was a master of emotional manipulation and control. Rachel played on the delicate balance of sexual impulse and love. She had cast herself as the wronged vulnerable divorcee—no doubt to attract my naïve sympathy.

Rachel's conversations that evening and most evenings after, were punctuated with innuendos about how few good men were available and how in that regard, it was acceptable, indeed necessary, to tell the not so infrequent untruth—i.e., lies. As if imparting State secrets, Rachel looked me square in the eyes under the moon's gaze and whispered: "What you don't know won't hurt you," and then asked, "don't you agree?" I gathered she assumed I was cut from the same sanctified cloth. She seemed oblivious of how indelicate her comments were, particularly under the circumstance of our advancing courtship. This for Rachel was intimate conversation; certainly those wiser than I might have perceived her comments as reflective of a lack of probity.

A couple of weeks later, I received an unexpected call from Rachel one Thursday afternoon, "Had to come into the city unexpectedly." She leisurely but firmly instructed, "Why don't you pack your weekend bag and we can head upstate to the barn." "I like pleasant surprises," I replied, "but sorry to sound like a wet blanket, I unfortunately have work responsibilities that I cannot abandon." My response engendered neither empathy nor any sense of concern beyond her impulsive desires. This incident was not dissimilar to events after our barbecue. She asked me bluntly once, "What's with all your friends?" As if friends were somehow ballast to be discarded overboard once their utility was exhausted. In Rachel's mind, you spend time with friends only to look for "copy", sex or other selfish pecuniary rewards. Having prematurely declared my love for Rachel in my initial exuberance for her entertaining charms and warm smile, it was unfortunately now too late for me. I had been masterfully ensnared in her elaborately woven emotional cobweb with the carelessly extravagant promise of more.

I had almost fainted on my maiden visit to the barn after a hike undertaken on an empty stomach on a blazing hot day. Rachel showed appropriate concern: "Here's some water, we don't want you to die," she said leaning over me. I read her concern as genuine and not that of a rich cynical property owner keen to avoid insurance liability for a dead body on the premises. Recovered sufficiently, and now sitting together in the sun by the pool, she asked me to read her aloud E.B. White's book, *Here is New York*, which I brought with me as a gift. I thought this was a little self-indulgent but at the same time very sweet. We were having a fulsome summer exploring the Hudson Valley together and frolicking by her pool. We hiked, danced merrily at the elegant Belgian inspired *Spiegeltent* at Bard College with local hipsters swaying and gyrating, attended the local Shakespeare Festival and visited many innovative restaurants that dotted the valley.

Rachel informed me she had told her parents about us—I was therefore instructed to expunge my Facebook status: single. It seemed that our relationship was filled with promise. But as the weeks passed, I slowly began to grasp that Rachel's promises were illusionary and her temperament would prove as unpredictable as the sun's solar flares. She became more and more enigmatic and unfamiliar. The glibness of her charm began to surface but I had not yet unraveled the puzzle that was Rachel.

It was sometime in late-June when she announced:

"I am having a big party on Labor Day. It's a fun event I do every year. Some years I've had up to a hundred guests on the property. Guests sleep in the open barn and camp in the fields."

"You mean like Woodstock?" I said with a tinge of incredulity; Rachel was fond of bombast.

"Yes, without the live music," she beamed enthusiastically.

As August approached, I received a mass email invitation in my Facebook inbox. This struck me as a trifle odd, a very impersonal choice of correspondence to your boyfriend. A few days later Rachel asked in passing if I wanted to invite any of my friends. It was less of an invitation than a mechanical statement. The same evening Rachel inadvertently let slip that many guests had declined her invitation. For my part, I was reticent; partly because I was unlikely to make it to the event myself since I was planning to take my children to Europe on vacation around that time. My plans had been concluded in May, before Rachel and I began dating. In any event, Rachel had already reassured me that despite our mutual commitments to our offspring, once school was underway, she would be spending much more time with me in the City. She seemed sincere in her desire and I was too naive to believe otherwise.

The day of the party soon arrived. I had flown back from Europe to be in attendance since it also coincided with Rachel's birthday. I felt it was important to be there for her. That afternoon, we welcomed the first guests, Peter and John, a delightful gay couple who were also from the countryside. Rachel did not introduce me and it was unclear if they knew I was her boyfriend—even if only in my head. We took a hike together and explored the property. I mentioned Rachel and I planned to attend the upcoming Toronto International Film Festival (TIFF) which stopped John in mid-stride. John seemed surprised and puzzled as to the nature of my relationship with Rachel, who had walked on ahead with Peter.

John happened to be a huge Anglophile, like me, which provided a natural bond. It transpired we also had a mutual theatrical friend, a former lover of John's, who was now deceased. So we were able to pleasantly continue our hike in animated conversation, leaving all matters of Rachel unspoken.

Other guests soon arrived. Rachel reverted to her shadow self and once again conveniently did not introduce me. Perhaps she wanted me to take charge, to play the boyfriend role unannounced in that unmistakable masculine way. I felt more like an uninvited guest than Rachel's boyfriend. Most invited guests had no idea if I was that evening's help or the host's partner. One guest even made light that he and his wife should linger longer in case I should decide to stay into the evening presumably with the hope of ending up in bed with the dutiful host. Other guests attempted to deduce my status by a process of elimination counting beds and who slept where. This was not an easy exercise since some like Rachel and myself, went to bed when pitch darkness had fallen on the barn and rose early. That

Promises—A Weekend in the Country

morning three humorous and entertaining guests, my favorites, led by John, enquired mischievously:

"Did you sleep in the tree-bed?" They were referring to the host's bed. I paused briefly; guests were frolicking by the pool as we sat on Adirondack chairs gazing into the lovely fields in the distance to the chatter of birds. I nodded, yes, discretely; Rachel's secret was now our secret, to the apparent foreboding of my now sympathetic audience. They knew how the story of our coupling would end. They understood far better than I the psychological complexities of my girlfriend and her checkered dating history.

In bed that night, after almost all of the guests had departed, a frosty Rachel unexpectedly unleashed a tirade of abuse:

"Why didn't you lend a hand washing dishes at the party?"

"Your behavior is unacceptable and appallingly rude!"

"You think you're polite but you are not!"

"Is washing dishes beneath you?" she yelled.

"How can you have lived in America so long and not know what to do?" This was the *coup de grâce*.

The ferocity of Rachel's disapprobation shocked me and turned my Labor Day weekend unexpectedly upside-down. At first I was at a loss to comprehend the extent of her anger and the fury in her face. After all, this was a minor misunderstanding about roles and expectations in a new multi-facetted relationship.

"This is not the first time," Rachel repeated. "There's a pattern," she was building momentum for the final fatal blow.

"We are too different for this relationship to work," she said with an ironic tone.

"You couldn't even set the table correctly!"

A weak blow if ever there was one delivered to a jet-lagged man. She had more insults but elected for now to hold her fire deeming me sufficiently wounded at this point. Other notable claims later leveled against me were that I was: too urbane, i.e., not given to farming by nature, as if this were a crime; took unduly long showers—a water waster; and to add insult to injury, changed towels daily. I did not share communal towels by the pool, preferring instead to unwrap and use new ones—including those being saved for more meaningful occasions like Christmas. Rachel was clearly keeping count of my perceived antediluvian transgressions and she let me know this in no uncertain terms. Bruised from my admonishment, I lay in her astonishing indoor tree bed, in the mezzanine loft of the barn, positioned in front of enormous picture windows, with the cool night breeze and mosquitoes buzzing, staring deep into the star filled night, looking for a logical explanation. It was a twilight zone moment; the awkward gap between cultural thinking and resultant contested narratives—so I thought. I met with these disconnects from time-to-time and knew they can only be bridged if partners are willing to concede ground. Communication, emotional management and acceptance of cultural differences were paramount to successfully navigate our discord. Rachel was oblivious to the fact that I worked hard all evening to keep her guests entertained and their glasses full. I even helped to erect a tent in the field outside the barn with a charming Israeli couple who had earlier revealed their recent engagement, as unbeknownst to me my girlfriend and other guests apparently relentlessly loaded and unloaded the dishwasher. I had misjudged Rachel. I made the fatal mistake of taking her seriously, i.e., deeming her normal—not maladjusted—and letting down my guard in the process. My instinctive compassion for her left me vulnerable. I was in that dangerous juncture between falling in love and the abrupt unhappiness unrequited love can cause. Rachel knew this and brazenly seized upon it.

Something had changed in my week long absence in Europe. On the eve of Rachel's birthday, I was awarded the honorable boot. In my English mode far from the stereotypical brash New York style—I coyly explained to Rachel:

"I wish you had introduced me as your boyfriend at the party, it would have made the evening less complicated. It would have also been helpful if you let me know you wanted me to take care of the dishes." She in turn grudgingly said, "Yes, I did not manage the situation well," but gave no clue to her inner thoughts. She seemed oblivious of the hurt she had caused. I asked her:

"Is there someone else?"

She said, "No," softly, with eyes averted and without conviction.

She continued coolly:

"We are not compatible. Compatibility can only occur at great expense to your inner core."

By "inner core," I presumed she meant my English sensibility—my scruples. I looked her tenderly in the eye. I sensed a rehearsed air—this speech had been delivered many times before.

I made the best of a very confusing situation. I left promptly the next morning, her birthday. Before we fell asleep, she asked me to stay, which I thought strange. I woke early, retrieved Rachel's birthday presents from my suitcase and presented them to her with a gentle kiss on the cheek while squeezing her large delightful hands. I hoped she liked the gifts. She seemed unmoved despite the fact that they were handpicked after frantic transatlantic text consultation with her during a frenetic family holiday.

The one remaining guest woke as I was heading for the door.

"You are not staying?" she enquired quizzically, seeing me with bag packed at my side. Supposedly a good friend, she did not seem to relish the thought of being left alone with Rachel.

"Sadly have to leave," I replied, "but hope you will make the birthday special for Rachel."

Rachel insisted, rather touchingly I thought—on making me a slice of my favorite raisin toast, like a loving wife, to tide me over for the cab ride to the train station. Meanwhile, the cab driver waited idling in the pebbled driveway.

Seated in the almost empty carriage on my Labor Day train ride back to Manhattan, I wondered if I had inadvertently crashed Rachel's party with my transatlantic interpretation of a helping hand. Now I recollect she did seem a trifle surprised that I RSVP'd so quickly. I was initially supposed to be away for the event but changed my holiday dates to be there. The reality was that she had no intention of a long-term relationship beyond a summer fling. My shelf-life had expired in Rachel's rapidly revolving romantic carousel.

Rachel's emotional void was both haunting and chilling. Our differences provided a convenient excuse for a less than gracious exit. We had planned that week to attend the US Open tennis championships and a film festival in Toronto, for which I had snagged tickets through a friend for a screening of a new film, as part of the celebrations for Rachel's birthday. Once dismissed, I had to cancel all these arrangements including flights and a hotel room all recently booked by me for Rachel's benefit. She did not care even a jot about any resulting inconvenience—lost hotel deposits, wasted air tickets and disappointed friends, who had arranged for our presence in the screening events with the Hollywood cast. It was almost as if she was entirely disassociated from the unraveling events. There was also a mildly sadistic triumphant air about her countenance. I believed innocently with my Commonwealth sensibility, that the combination of our shared Catholic upbringing and Harvard Ivy League values somehow would make the rules of engagement honest. My romantic notions should have been dispelled relatively early in our courtship when Rachel said, "Wow! You are very romantic," which I took as a compliment not knowing it was meant as a putdown—a statement of how misplaced my feelings were given her transient aspirations for us.

Now wiser, in my last communication to Rachel, I told her I would be glad to remain friends, so long as the friendship was not "gloss." She responded indignantly, "I can't imagine you think I operate with gloss." "*Operate*," I thought was a strange choice of words. But it described very aptly how she did indeed conduct her affairs.

All told, my time with Rachel was mostly sobering. She was blessed with a high IQ and conversely morbidly low Emotional IQ; she knew how to mimic love but could not love. I had dodged a near fatal bullet. The damage would have been more profound had we been together longer and if the bullet had lodged in my heart. Also mercifully, our children were never in the picture, something Rachel managed with remarkable finesse and the *nous* of an experienced player.

Londris—Europe's Cool New City

Samuel Johnson is reputed to have said: "When a man is tired of London, he is tired of life; for there is in London all that life can afford." But London is no longer London, just as Paris is no longer Paris. It took great imagination and enterprise, but today we have *Londris*, a conjunction of London and Paris.

These great cities sit at opposite poles between a rapid rail-link that runs from city center to city center. They function for some as co-joined twin cities. Frequent Eurostar trains bring you through the English Channel via the tunnel euphemistically referred to as the *Chunnel* in as little as two hours sixteen minutes, not much longer than it takes to get to Birmingham in the Midlands from London. The *Chunnel* is a cultural bridge that brings the French and English together in a way never seen before. Napoleon had dreamed of invading England by tunnel, it is now a reality, albeit a cultural invasion rather than the military takeover he envisaged.

Chunnel passengers represent a diverse array of people from all walks of life. They include: frequent business commuters, vacationers, and international travelers from America, China, Japan and elsewhere, students taking day excursions and lovers off for a romantic weekend. Once on land, The Eurostar, *La Grande Vitesse*, an air conditioned bullet, hurtles rapidly across the French and English countryside at 180 miles per hour. Passengers gaze from the comfort of their seats at bucolic fields, farms and livestock, and Kent's distinctive *Oast Houses* with their white slanting conical roofs (kilns for drying hops for brewing), without the inconvenience of breaking a sweat in Continental traffic.

The opening of the Eurostar *Chunnel* in 1994, heralded a new dawn for how Londoners and Parisians see themselves. In between then and now, an armada of 400,000, French nationals have relocated to England to sample the eccentric delights of its capital London. South Kensington is becoming a facsimile of a Paris Arrondissement.

In London they are able to escape their own cultural tyranny at home—the *particular* strictures of French society—as well as punitive taxes on the well off. They've brought with them French baguettes and in the process have revolutionized British palates. A new type of Englishman and woman is emerging, giving rise to hybrid cultures. These new French expatriates are as comfortable in their home cities as they are in London. They relish London's cosmopolitan spirit and mercantile pursuits, so much so, in fact, that for them, London and Paris are but one gigantic urbane conurbation—*Londris*. Here they are able to abandon the bourgeois orthodoxies of both societies—to emerge with a fresh cultural identity comfortably straddling both sides of the tunnel.

London has for many centuries been a cosmopolitan hub at the center of trade, commerce and finance. It is England's cultural jewel. In more recent years it has also become a playground for the super-rich—wives of Russian oligarchs and their husbands, former military dictators, Arab petro-carbon billionaire Sheikhs and radical clerics. Its cosmopolitan revival, some, like *Monty Python* comedian John Cleese, argue, is denuding London of the essence of its character—it's Britishness—pork pies and pints of bitter in its ubiquitous timeless pubs. This is a view I share, but a situation I applaud.

London has become England's singularly most important economic asset next to Her Majesty the Queen. England's ancient guilds—commercial societies for grocers, drapers, haberdashers, skinners, fishmongers, tailors, scriveners and apothecaries—are now complemented by three star *Michelin* restaurants. This is in addition to other bastions of French culture, like Paul's eateries and florists in the French fashion—some worthy of the *Meilleurs Ouvriers de France (MOF)* designation reserved for France's finest craftsmen and craftswomen.

The cranes that dot central London's skyline, attest to the city's renaissance. Rising property prices continue to crowd out native Londoners, intensifying the city's international character as rich foreign property buyers' swoop-in from France and elsewhere. Paris by contrast has a skyline bereft of the cranes that symbolize change. Emphasis instead is placed on polishing and restoration of monuments and landmarks that give the city its distinct charm and reinforce its moniker as The City of Light. Unlike London, Paris properties for the most part represent dwellings and treasured homes not speculative financial assets.

London's ascendency over Paris in the *Chunnel* poles is symbolized by the glittering cathedral of St. Pancras International Station, where passengers are discharged into its vast lively concourses of shops, restaurants, bars and grand modernized Victorian railway hotel, to efficiently connect with London's underground network, the oldest such network in the world. *Gare du Nord,* the French alighting and boarding point, by contrast, seems to embody creeping urban decay that is blighting Paris—shabby rather than shabby chic. This same blight perhaps is urging some of its citizens to board the Eurostar to escape to the once dull and stodgy environs of a revitalized London. Of course, while preferring London's invigorating lifestyle, they have the security of knowing they can quickly pop-back on the Eurostar in search of their favorite and most obscure French cheese which may not have yet found a home in London.

Paris seems on a collision course with the troubled *banlieues* (suburbs) that house the city's hidden poor immigrant communities beyond the *Périphérique*—the ring road that circles the well-to-do Paris that most tourists see. At *Gare du Nord, beaux Paris* and the *banlieues* appear to be already acquainted. The only edge over St. Pancras that *Gare du Nord* offers, is *Terminus Nord Brasserie,* a superb classic railway restaurants nearby with immaculate service, starched white table clothes and a fleet of white and black attired waitpersons to rapidly dispense tasty morsels to fortify travelers ahead of their cross *Chunnel* trip. Here you will feel like you are living *Brassaï's* famous photograph, *Couple D'Amoureux dans un Café, Paris, 1932.*

Station restaurants are often among the finest in their simple classic gastronomic elegance. This is one of France's many secrets.

The welcome at both ends is reflective of the character of each nation. In London you are greeted by formidable customs and immigration personnel who, it seems, are still expecting an unannounced Continental invasion. In Paris, gates are more open with selective and discreet monitoring of errant passengers by the occasional *gendarmes*. Invasion seems less a concern among the French, who are gaining insight into the benefits of a less bigoted and ossified world at the other end of the *Chunnel*. London, despite its Anglicized self, for the most part, welcomes and embraces culture from outside that enriches its social fabric. Quintessential London is today synonymous with its cosmopolitan cultures. You will not find wholesale bans on burkas there, for instance, as you will in France. Nor will you find codes of law that limit working hours to 35 hours a week.

Beyond *Gare du Nord*, is Paris—its infinite smug charm, *terrasse cafés* with genius *maître d's*, who seat and arrange beautiful guests so as to create a spectacular human floral bouquet and delightful inner courtyards—accessed by a security code that releases the lock to the sound of a gentle signature Parisian click, which allows you to open the heavy glossy, dark-green, wooden door.

As a dear expatriate *Londrisian* friend of mine says when asked to comment on London's rejuvenation, "The best thing about London is Paris!"

Africa's Waking Giant—Where Next?

News coverage of Nigeria nowadays seems almost exclusively devoted to terrorist acts by *Boko Haram* to the extent that recently a friend's mother asked me: "It must be hellishly frightening with all that heavy fighting in the streets." It was news to her that the vast majority of the country's 160 million people in Africa's giant conduct their daily activities peaceably and unmolested by terror.

In its buzzing metropolis Lagos, commuters leave for work as early as 4:00 am to miss the city's renowned *Go-Slow* traffic jams. By 6:00 am, the streets are bustling with local and interstate mass transit buses, mini vans, decrepit yellow taxis with friendly drivers and motorcycles, as well as private vehicles. Smartly uniformed school children can be seen perhaps an hour or so later. Office workers cheerily greet each other on the street, while busy housewives and houseboy dash to shop at colorful flourishing markets, like, *Balogun and Lekki*, and the city's fashionable new malls. Weddings and other lively celebrations are to be found in compounds in most neighborhoods. Party guests eat local flavor-filled dishes like *jollof* rice and stew and drink the country's famed Star Lager Beer, while dancing to the rhythmic beat of West African music well into the night. There is vibrancy, a gaiety in many parts of Nigeria, which seems to be missed in international press reporting. Most Nigerians are oblivious of random attacks in the remote north of the country. Surely there are other newsworthy events in Nigeria, like efforts to avoid a social tinderbox by promoting much delayed development in the north of the country? There is a growing acknowledgment among the country's southern citizenry that development and opportunities have lagged in the northern part of the nation. Nigerians recognize that these imbalances must be redressed to stem discontent among disaffected and economically marginalized youth, attracted to terror in the absence of meaningful alternative occupations.

There simply is too much trashy press of questionable merit on almost all of the 54 countries that make up Africa, a continent which is the world's second most populous and the second largest by land mass. Africa has an image problem. It still seems to be depicted—in pictures and headlines—and in most media sources, as a savage continent interminably divided against itself. This singularly negative image presumably ensures papers are sold. Africa needs to find talent and resources to correct hackneyed cliché, which still define the continent in many people's minds. Having visited Nigeria recently, I can confirm that judging from events at the luxury Radisson Blu Anchorage Hotel in the commercial capital Lagos, the country is quietly buzzing with Western and Chinese visitors, as well as those from many parts of Africa and beyond. I did not witness any incidents of violence during my week's visit beyond a single case of mild road rage—a brief motoring altercation featuring unpleasant hand gestures from the driver of the offending vehicle. And certainly no random acts of gun rampage that seem to be endemic in today's America. Africa like America is many things. That's not to say there are not troubles in Nigeria but the exclusive focus by the international press leaves an impression that the country is a war zone, which is far removed from the actual realities on the ground. *The New York Times* in particular, approaches Africa with remarkably consistent narrow lenses which serve to keep its readers in the realms of Conrad's *Heart of Darkness*.

While in Nigeria, I visited both Abuja and Lagos and witnessed an air of excitement I have not seen in the country since the swinging petrodollar days of the mid-1970s. In Abuja, executives and senior government officials toil late into the evenings in their new skyscraper offices. This reminded me of my early visits to Brazil in the late-1990s, during its own social and political reforms, which galvanized its economy. The city's power brokers are said to conduct most of their dealings in the late hours. There seems to be less frenzy this time round and perhaps more purpose.

The staggering gap between rich and poor persists although a wafer thin middle class seems to be emerging with the consumer habits of their prosperous and significantly less numerous elite cadres. Young faces abound, many with little to do other than watch the rich pass by with gloating envy. Becoming rich appears to be a full-time occupation for those who are not. Even the most unlikely and wretched city dwellers talk of dreams of owning "PJs"—not silk pajamas, but private jets! The *Nigeria Dream* puts the *American Dream* to shame in its ambition. It is worth noting that Nigerians occupy three of the top five-billionaire spots including number one in the continent's rich list (which of course excludes former dictators). It may also surprise some to learn that the richest Black person on the planet is not American but is Nigerian. With estimated wealth of $20.8 billion, industrialist Aliko Dangote is the world's 43rd richest person according to *Forbes*. Oprah Winfrey tops the list for African-Americans with a net worth of $2.9 billion.

I also had the opportunity to meet some of the country's leading business, financial and technical elite charged with managing change and modernization, as well as one of the country's top literary luminaries. Distinguished author and MacArthur "Genius Grant" winner, Chimamanda Ngozi Adichie, asked in a car ride to Abuja's, Nnamdi Azikiwe International Airport, how I would describe Nigerians abroad. I said they are chameleons; proud, patriotic, and proficient at adapting—camouflaging their Nigerian-ness, sometimes out of necessity to counter rampant prejudice and stereotypes. I added that they were, excelling in their newfound environments. I did not have an opportunity to share with her what I heard one morning at my New York newspaper store. There I found three young men chatting: an Indian, a Nigerian and an African-American. Each shared a story about their father. The Nigerian told a tale of when his father first came to America as a student and showed up for work as a part-time dishwasher in his best interview suit, which was ruined by the end of the day. He did not repeat this mistake again. Driven by pride and necessity he redoubled his efforts to complete his university studies and to gain his pharmacist qualifications in order to escape the unfamiliar heat in the kitchens.

In Nigeria, I was impressed by the energy and technical ability of the dedicated professionals I met—many of who were educated at some of the most prestigious institutions in the world and have returned to Nigeria because they see opportunity. Interestingly, a recent Yale study shows that students of Nigerian ancestry comprise almost 25% of black students at Harvard Business School. I could not help but think that perhaps someday Nigeria might morph into Africa's first *Creative Economy* (Nigeria's fledgling *Nollywood* is the world's third largest film industry behind Hollywood and *Bollywood* in India).

I did not meet with any of the country's current generation of political leaders. Given what I saw, there was a disconnect between the remarkable abilities of these individuals and the ordered chaos I was witnessing. I could only imagine what extraordinary achievements they might accomplish if the State was less corrupt and more enabling. Nigeria unfortunately is a nation adrift, still held hostage by a rich few who feed off the State and cling closely to power. The country sorely needs a visionary leader. Nigeria needs the type of statesman or woman who can delight the people and usher in transformative change, one with guts, integrity and ambition. Instead, those at the top of the heap continue to choke an articulate elite and a young ambitious population hungry for change. Some of these, alas, are only keen for a chance at the roulette wheel. These rogue mentality types are slowly being flushed out of the system. Corruption remains endemic although its odious impact is being recognized and there is some semblance of state inspired public relations to staunch its march.

Transparency is a huge challenge for the State and the culture of the "Big Man" the *"Oga"* is still omnipresent. Nigeria has not yet found its selfless combination of Mahatma Gandhi, Nelson Mandela,

Margaret Thatcher, J. F. Kennedy and Steve Jobs, to put it on a path that will fulfill its vast promise. Uruguay's leader, President José Mujica might serve as a model. *The Guardian* reports, that he eschews the state palace for a farmhouse; flies economy, donates most of his salary to worthy causes and drives a modest old Volkswagen Beetle. Such an exemplary selfless leader would no doubt improve and enrich the material lives of many Nigerians. Perhaps he or she might even instill a culture of transparency and civic orderliness in government.

Nigerians, more than half of whom are under the age of twenty-three, desperately need sound leadership—credible individuals with backbone who are able to lead by example. They must come equipped with fresh constructive ideas that are measurable and can inspire citizens to act selflessly. Nigeria has abundant human and natural resources to fulfill the dreams of its entire people. Dogged commitment and accountability are needed to deliver a better life that Nigerians desire and deserve: adequate food, running water, electricity, education, health care, clean and reliable public transportation, security and a functioning infrastructure.

Nigeria is much younger than America, a mere 50 years old as a country and a century as a geographic construct. America by contrast has almost two-and-a-half centuries of nationhood behind it, including its own transformative civil war. Nigerians are impatient for change, in an age where the so called BRICs—Brazil, Russia, India and China—have demonstrated, much can be accomplished in a relatively short time with committed leadership. Nigerians, rightly, are not ready for the human rights and labor law compromises that have propelled China's growth but they are more than sophisticated enough to realize that so much more can be accomplished beyond failed successive governments and bankrupt leadership. With a population expected by the United Nations to pass that of the US by 2050 and to match China by the turn of the century, Nigeria remains a country for the future and has been anointed a member of the MINT (Mexico, Indonesia, Nigeria and Turkey) Economies believed to be the next wave after the BRICs. It is a country with heft and momentum, one that can deliver with focused political will.

Bet on Nigeria. Despite its idiosyncratic political leadership, Nigeria is too well endowed and Nigerians are too proud and industrious to be left behind with current domestic problems unresolved. You will be amply rewarded if you are prudent and patient.

Dharma (Moral Imperative)

I have awakened belatedly to the powerful significance of cultural relativism and its immense impact on our lives. Dharma, or universal moral imperatives, affect how we respond to many situations and whether, the impulses underlying our decisions are communal driven or individual based. Dharma in our lives can be the source of considerable frustration when we find ourselves in groups or societies with opposing moral reasoning. This can cause confusion since their ethics may not match our own and may in fact be diametrically opposed. I was born in a communal society where many norms and mores are determined and set by intricate kinship and family arrangements. I then moved and grew up in England, a society, where those social arrangements and values, were much weaker. I now live in America, where individual rights and freedoms are paramount and where communal values often take a backseat to individual expression. These three differing moral landscapes provide fertile ground for confusion.

Reconciling and understanding the basis for our decisions and those of others is a complex endeavor that requires extraordinary clarity of thought and self-awareness. Moral imperative impels us to act in various ways under a variety of circumstances. For instance, in American culture it is okay to put your parents in a retirement home while in India it would be an abhorrent morally shameful act resulting in social ostracism by kinfolk. In many cultures moral duties and social responsibility are inextricably bound. Here in America, individual desire usually trumps collective expectations.

We must therefore look inside our heads and those of others we associate with to understand how we fit relatively on the Dharma (moral imperative) spectrum. Without doing so, we may be exposed, like a fish out of water, to disorientation, and unexplained vertigo that can have socially disastrous consequences. You may be left, as I was initially in America, asking in the face of patent injustice: 1) why you appear to be the only person publicly outraged,

Dharma (Moral Imperative)

asking why the community is not up in arms, and 2) why the wronged individual has been left to fend for themselves to seek redress for a harm we all know is evident, through the courts of law rather than through the collective moral force of the community. On many occasions, I witnessed wrongs and asked myself, "Where is the sense of collective shame—of community?" For example, in my early days in New York, I observed a landlord openly terrorizing tenants to force them to leave their Brownstone in order to convert their dwelling into a luxury condominium. Rumor has it, that he even arranged the mugging in the tight entryway of the oldest tenant, who was lodged in the coveted garden apartment. After which, this poor widower was left in constant fear—forced to surrender and move from his marital home of fifty years. Tenants with the means fled and left those without, like the old man, to fend for themselves.

One might similarly ask why we appear to hate segments of our own society and why we leave poor people, women and minorities at the periphery in today's America? They have an equal right to vote and to protection of the State and its people. Equally— it is hard to fathom a national shut-down in protest of citizens not receiving affordable health care, something people take for granted in many other countries like, Canada, France and England. Not so long ago, I was on a business trip to France and was astonished that the hotel gladly summoned a physician *gratis* to tend to my dreadful flu in my room and to prescribe medication at nominal expense. There is to my mind—i.e., my sense of Dharma—a shocking paralysis in America's communal behavior, an acquiescence of moral imperatives to reckless amoral individuals and a hapless faceless authority—the State.

For us to comprehend others and for them to comprehend us in their moral thoughts, it is vital to understand where they and we, so to speak, are coming from. In the absence of this understanding, we become ships passing in the night with incomprehension on both sides. Moral realities of the same experiences and situations will accordingly differ, sowing the seeds for dissatisfaction and possible disharmony. In the extreme case, misplaced Dharma can lead to a victim mentality, a persecution complex and even beyond, to mental illness, when someone feels morally disassociated and not understood. In short, leaving the individual confused and alienated from the values of the society they find themselves in. I know of at least one such instance. A Ghanaian woman, a Harvard College graduate I knew only slightly became mentally disentangled and began to wander and sleep on the streets of Cambridge. I am not sure what eventually became of her, although the African alumni did try to rally to her aid. My parents had told me of many such instances in England, where new arrivals from a variety of cultures were unable to reconcile their communal moral imperatives with the looser, and more fluid social morals of their newfound hosts. Due to the complications of their circumstances, they were unable to find sanctuary within their own communities.

Thankfully, there seems to be consensus on some broad issues across cultures of moral imperative, "thou shalt not kill," for example.

Navigating or searching for our Dharma is a modern imperative. Discerning how to act appropriately, within the context of universal morality—balancing duty versus desire in different cultural settings, without upending your own moral anchor—is the dilemma of Dharma for each of us, particularly if you are cosmopolitan.

TALES

Isabella

Some years ago, relieved after my usual madcap airport dash, I sat waiting to board my flight to Paris from New York's JFK. An elegant Air France agent decked in a formfitting powder-blue dress with matching Chanel-like jacket greeted me at the check-in desk. She gave my passport and my ticket an obligatory examination. Then she politely weighed and checked my single piece of luggage onto the idle conveyer belt. Air France had informed me some weeks earlier that I was one of their most frequent transatlantic flyers. My reward was a special dedicated agent to take care of my bookings. Next I waited not so patiently for my boarding-pass which was crisply handed over in a flash. The agent wished me *"Bon Voyage"* with a playful clandestine smile. I was on my way.

Air France has this charming habit of not telling you you've been upgraded until directed to your seat by the cabin crew. The immense psychological effect of this moment cannot be understated.

Feeling suitably elevated in my sumptuous first-class window-seat, I arranged my travel accoutrements: iPod, newspapers (*The New York Times, Financial Times,* and *Wall Street Journal*—the former and latter American broadsheets were to be discarded immediately under the seat in front in case of a terrorist incident) and a novel, *A Suitable Boy*, by Vikram Seth. The brick-like tome added pounds to my already colossal hand-luggage, which created some peculiar resentment on my part towards opening its pages. I tossed an assorted handful of magazines on the empty seat next to mine, none of which, I might add, were likely to see any attention until several hours into the eight hour flight. More likely than not, once airborne, sleep would follow. Air France's finest complimentary champagne would aid my pending siesta.

I count myself lucky to be among those travelers for whom nothing could be more heavenly than sleeping above the clouds at 40,000 feet in the fuselage of a giant speeding bullet. I feel very close to the gods when flying. Initial takeoff nerves aside, flying engenders in me a sense of complete and utter calm. No phones, emails, or unexpected knocks at my door to contend with. So, ahead of takeoff, I powered-up my cellphone to say goodnight to my daughter, and as if by providence, at that very precise moment a flight attendant announced: "Ladies and gentlemen, please fasten your seat belt and switch off all electronic devices." We were shortly aloft and I felt that champagne-induced giddy excitement that flying to Paris always stirs. Images of the smart cafes of the Left Bank and the civilized limestone surroundings of the 9th Arrondissement, where I would be staying at the *Hotel Montalembert*, filled my mind.

I was soon fast asleep with my seat fully reclined. No point in half-measures when you have been upgraded to first-class! After my customary two hour snooze, I woke to eat the airline's offering of crab salad and *foie gras*. I washed down my meal with two demi-glasses of *Bordeaux* followed by equal measures of *Perrier*. Sated, I settled back to read the delightful in-flight magazine, one of the few airline publications worth reading. In true French fashion, Air France has a men's magazine and a women's magazine. The French rather sensibly understand that there are differences which have to be catered for accordingly. The women's magazine is more interesting since it covers all the latest Parisian trends including fashion and where to stay, eat, shop, and to see and be seen. As I read, an advertisement caught my eye. I paused before turning the page to look at a picture of a very attractive woman with cherub like features. She had raven colored hair cut in a short chic Roman-style. It was one of those beguiling faces that stays eternally imprinted in your mind. This beautiful woman seemed somehow familiar yet unfamiliar. I glanced out of the window at the clouds, my brain racing frantically to see if I could recall who she was.

As I contemplated, the seat in front of mine slowly reclined 180 degrees into a bed. I gazed down upon the supine body, and the most wondrous vision. I glanced back at the magazine and then back at the goddess lying gracefully on the seat in front of me, fast asleep curled up angelically like a new born baby. It took a few seconds for me to realize that it was indeed the face in the magazine. Isabella Rossellini! I tried to contain my excitement as best as I could. Tingles ran excitedly up and down my spine. I reclined my own seat with a (false) air of nonplussed indifference.

The rest of the flight was uneventful until we approached CDG (Charles de Gaulle International Airport), also referred to as *"Roissy"*—the area in which the airport is located—by locals of a certain era. I pondered if I should refer to JFK airport as Idlewild from now on. The flight crew discreetly approached Ms. Rossellini. A female attendant with equine looks and penetrating green eyes nervously whispered: "Madame Rossellini will you require a VIP car." Smiling back gently, Madame Rossellini politely demurred and walked gracefully down the aisle, disembarking by way of the aft stairs to board one of those tiresome white angular Air France buses to the connecting terminal. I lingered in my seat but no one came to enquire if I would need VIP car service, perhaps a bit of a stretch I reflected, given that I was an "upgrade," so I too disembarked into the Parisian autumn morning chill.

Isabella seemed quite at ease with us common folk, and took her seat on the bus without fanfare, looking barely ruffled from her night's slumber. Her attention seemed elsewhere. She was gazing through the bus windows at a multitude of rabbits bounding energetically in and out of warrens on the grassy verge beside the runways. The rabbits were clearly oblivious to the presence of a celebrity in their midst. We all looked on, I was fascinated by the rabbits while hoping the driver would close the bus doors and turn up the heat. Meanwhile, a mesmerizing array of crisscrossing vehicles glided purposefully across the tarmac in an intricate choreographed dance. Like the rabbits, they swept under the belly and wings of stationary aircraft and the giant black pneumatic *Michelin* tires of other taxiing jetliners.

On arrival at the designated gate, Madam Rossellini silkily alighted from the bus and followed the *"Correspondance"* (Transfer) signs up the escalators with what seemed like the entire CDG Air France staff in her wake. The rest of us mortals were left to fend for ourselves.

Parisian Tales—You Still Don't Smoke!

While waiting in the chic Air France lounge at CDG, my American colleague, Chuck, spotted a young Parisian man busily smoking under the No-Smoking sign. Infuriated, he approached the fashionably attired man, who was perched delicately on his seat with legs neatly folded and a cigarette firmly clasped between his index finger and thumb. "Sir we're seated in a designated No-smoking area," he said firmly in his best French accent. The young man looked up slowly, smiled, and said with a mischievous defiant grin: "This is France!" while blowing a plume of *Gauloises* smoke in my colleague's face. He then casually unruffled his copy of *Le Figaro* and returned his attention to the sports section. Mouth agape my colleague looked on in bemused wonderment.

On another occasion, I was in from London having arrived for lunch on the TGV from Waterloo—before Eurostar service was moved to St. Pancras International. I was scheduled to have one of those fabulous gastronomic five-course French business lunches that alas are a relic of the past, like the *Citroën Deux Chevaux*. Consumption of several bottles of wine by guest and host was obligatory, starting with, in sequence: an aperitif, white wine, red wine, and finally dessert wine. All imbibed only after 1) a rigorous examination against the light and 2) a display of an array of pleasing facial gestures, tut-tutting and guttural tones denoting acceptance of the vintage.

In those days menus were exclusively in French and my host, who was also my client, would painstakingly translate every dish down to the method of preparation for each vegetable, as well as the provenance of individual herbs. Seasonality was also dwelled upon, since only local items in season were prepared and offered up. Dishes arrived one by one on virginal white plates, each gently caressed with utensils before being devoured with rapturous pleasure, unleashing a symphony of delicate flavors exploding deliciously on your palate. Our copious wine consumption seemed to do little to diminish the negotiating skills of my client. Quite the contrary, it seemed to sharpen his resolve and oddly his focus too. For me, on the other hand, unaccustomed to such mid-afternoon binges, each successive glass of wine, reduced my speech to incoherent babble which to the untrained ear might have been mistaken for the drawling twang of a *Gérard Depardieu* character from the Provinces.

On this occasion, after our gastronomic adventure, it was my client's habit to offer me a cigarette, which I declined. My *"Non merci"* was met with a belligerent and alarmed exclamation: "You still don't smoke!" said as if admonishing a ten-year old child who had again wet the bed. I had committed a mortal sin. The Continental divide was vast indeed. I looked down, suitably ashamed at my grave *faux pas*, and focused my attention squarely on polishing off the fine claret remaining in the bottom of my glass. This at least I could appreciate and translate without too much fuss.

"L'addition, s'il vous plait," my host announced to the waiter in the distance, while gesturing extravagantly with his hands in the air. The waiter hastily arrived with Parisian efficiency. A neatly printed bill was soon proffered on a silver platter. After some brief pleasantries, my jovial and agreeable host dispatched the waiter with a check swiftly and elegantly scribed in his own hand with a stubby polished black and gold lacquer *Montblanc* fountain pen. I offered to pick-up the tip but was brushed-off and reminded—*"Prix comprises!"*— That in France it is included; a couple of one-franc coins would suffice to show a courteous appreciation beyond the standard tip.

Lunch now concluded after almost four delightful hours, my client rose and bade me goodbye. Staggering ever so slightly with a confident gait, he exited to the street, lit a cigarette, gazed at the swirling carousel of mid-afternoon Paris and proceeded to totter gracefully down to the underground parking garage to retrieve his car. He waved a salute from his vehicle and drove his *Peugeot* in reckless Parisian fashion through busy traffic to his office to collect his briefcase for his next appointment—undoubtedly a *Cinq à Sept Liaison*.

Portmanteaus

Air France outdid itself with its benevolence to me one day. The first of several business class upgrades to *Concorde*! Ah 60,000 feet, the edge of space and even closer to the gods than on your average subsonic jetliner. It was glamorous, but I could never get over the feeling that I was on a Greyhound bus with high-rollers bound for Atlantic City or Las Vegas.

Boarding was always eventful and entertaining. A young lady, a first time supersonic traveler gushed:

"Ah isn't that Naomi Campbell!" Lushly beautiful, she was sitting still and uncharacteristically calm heading on a jaunt, as she frequently did, for lunch in New York.

"I think that's Michael Douglas," with the high powered investment banking couple, I happened to know through my former work life, who merged in a spectacular wedding in Nantucket last summer.

The narrow pencil-like fuselage was flanked by two rows of cream colored leather seats either side of a tiny aisle down which the meal service was rapidly dispensed on bone china plates by the refined elite from the Air France stables. There was barely time for food to be served and consumed before landing. No selection of latest movies here, what little space there was, had to be devoted to the numerous bottles of vintage champagne to be consumed by the celebrities on-board.

Oddly enough although there was officially no coach or business class on *Concorde*, the glitterati were usually seated in the front-rows for maximum effect while plebeian passengers like me were seated in the middle and back-rows. So much for French values of *liberty, equality* and *fraternity*.

Portmanteaus

Some rows behind me were Ellie-May and Royce traveling for the first time outside Oklahoma busily snapping photos of everything and everyone. They sat smiling gleefully as the afterburners were switched on for extra takeoff thrust. The engines roared loud and the plane shot into the air in rocket style at an acute angle. The exhilarating sensation of G-forces pinned bums and torsos extra firmly to their seats. All eyes were glued to the cabin information display, which showed temperature, altitude and velocity counting up as the supersonic aircraft's four afterburners were switched on once again for added thrust to take us past Mach 1.0. Flushed with a supersonic rush, the novices broke into a spontaneous chorus of hurrahs; clapping once the display was lit bright with the maximum cruising speed of Mach 2.0, twice the speed of sound. Ellie-May and Royce would be first among the novices onboard to have their picture taken next to the display. The cabin crew announced that our delta-winged bird had stretched as much as six inches due to the heat and expansion brought on by supersonic flight. Ellie-May particularly enjoyed the thrilling sight of the slight curvature of the earth from the plane's tiny windows and the trailing stream of mist on the edge of the delta wing. She had the satisfaction of knowing that only astronauts had ventured higher. Royce, clearly a man of no small means was pondering how many oil wells it would take to buy one of these small jets for his private use to shuttle on business between Oklahoma City and Dallas.

Sorry, I have to pause here. I need to go to the "Waterloo"—*toilette* or bathroom in English rhyming slang—before we begin our rapid descent into the earth's atmosphere. Using the toilet in *Concorde* required the dexterity of a limbo dancer and the patience of a saint since the sharply curving fuselage made it impossible to stand upright for most men other than dwarfs. The toilet or bathroom reminded me of *Alice in Wonderland*. Everything save for the toilet itself was in miniature, the taps and super-small beautifully machined steel air-vents were all very 1960s space-age. The fittings would not have been out of place on the once futuristic set for *Thunderbirds*, the TV show of yesteryear. I marveled at the technology and thought about transistor radios as I relieved myself and watched the bright yellow urine flowing down the shining stainless steel bowel.

Returning to my seat, I struck up conversation with the young woman seated next to me. This was highly unusual since I am usually seated next to an oversized Mongolian monk on pilgrimage to don't ask me where. She was a professional single mum by all accounts somehow involved in the fashion world. A few glasses of champagne later, as the plane literally rocketed into the sky, she began to relax and initiated the infernal New York game of: "Do you know?" It turned out that she was a vague acquaintance of a college friend of mine who had dabbled in Paris fashion and was now designing handbags for a New York fashion house. The higher the *Concorde* flew the closer she inched towards me apparently impervious of the fact that I had gone out of my way to explain that I was eagerly looking forward to seeing my other-half back in New York. She finally fell asleep on my shoulder. I did my best to pretend that all was okay, periodically ruffling my *Financial Times* newspaper to see if she could be dislodged like an unwanted barnacle stuck to a racing yacht's hull. I guess the combination of alcohol and the rarified air caused a loss of inhibitions which I knew would rapidly evaporate as the pilot announced, "We are beginning our descent into the Tri-state area…"

At the luggage carousal I exchanged flirting glances with Naomi, who must have mistaken me for an African potentate in my stylish *Cutler & Gross* sunglasses. Then I realized that she was exchanging flirting glances with an army of men busily scrambling behind me for the privilege of taking her numerous and ponderous pieces of *Louis Vuitton* luggage from the conveyor. The fact that she had two burly skycaps ready and waiting to haul her portmanteaus seemed of no matter.

The Countessa

We arrived in Rome's Leonardo da Vinci Fiumicino Airport at about six in the morning, after a thankfully uneventful flight, eager to make our way by rental car to Chianti where we had lodgings booked at a villa belonging to a local *Countessa*. We were on the holiday because a work colleague of my girlfriend belatedly had to cancel—so we became benefactors of a dream cut-price luxury Italian vacation. It was an inauspicious start to our vacation, since we had arrived on a public holiday which meant that all cars were already rented out. The luck alas of the uninformed American traveler keen to conquer the world on America's holiday schedule. Undeterred, we made our way by taxi to Rome's central train station where we managed to obtain train directions to Chianti.

We finally arrived exhausted at our destination at around midnight. Our host, the *Countessa*, was there to greet us.

"Hello, welcome to Chianti," she said in a monotone voice in crisp English. She was a petite woman with a worn tattered aristocratic air, not the effusive warmth one normally associates with Italians. But she did speak exceedingly good English albeit with a tony Italian inflection. The *Countessa*, despite her cold welcome, was clearly a worldly woman. She ushered us into the kitchen:

"Would you like some pasta?" she asked as a reluctant afterthought.

"Yes!" we responded in unison somewhat aghast that she could not comprehend that we had not eaten a single meal all day. "Some wine would be great too; it was a very thirsty train journey."

We had assumed that Chianti would have been hospitably offered without asking. The *Countessa* overcame her parsimonious streak and proffered:

"Would you like a bottle of [mediocre] wine with dinner?" She then abruptly announced, "Your rented villa is no longer available!"

I said, "You mean the private villa we have already paid for in advance."

"Yes, but I can offer you alternative accommodation in the main house." She was referring to her home.

We were honored and in any event too tired to protest further after a long arduous journey with our six-year old daughter. We thanked her profusely having expected to be tossed out on the street to fend for ourselves. We trundled wearily upstairs to our quarters for much needed sleep. But not for long. Our deep jet-lagged slumber was soon disturbed by the sound of music, raucous Italian teenagers and their friends arriving home after a party followed by admonitions to be quiet because there were unwanted guests in their home.

We slept little, but woke late. We made our way to the kitchen, where we were offhandedly informed: "Sorry you've missed breakfast!" The mean stone-faced matronly housekeeper was not disposed to oblige with some food for us, not even for our daughter. Thankfully the *Countessa* arrived and intervened. Some bread, butter and coffee was miraculously found to aid in the start of our day. We knew somehow there would be a price to be paid for this unexpected generosity. Further disappointment came when the *Countessa* informed us that: The swimming pool accompanying the villa we booked and paid for was also not going to be available. "Sorry!" Our dream vacation was in tatters and was fast turning into a nightmare.

That night as we wandered the corridors on our tiptoes for fear of disturbing the household, we bumped into the *Countessa's* spouse, a Malian musician who kindly offered us one of his CDs. "Enjoy your stay," he said in unconvincing halting English, in an odd mix of a French-Italian accent. Like the rabbit in *Alice in Wonderland*, he vanished silently through one of the many unmarked doors in the residence. This was an unexpected surprise. We were an interracial couple as well and we thought this common bond might ignite some warmth in the heart of the *Countessa* but none was forthcoming. The husband's own countenance indicated that he might also be there at the displeasure of the *Countessa*. She apparently liked our American dollars but not our presence. Renting helped her maintain the upkeep of her estate, but she clearly resented having guests in her home and wanted her privacy back for herself and her children.

The stress of creeping around their home became unbearable and we found ourselves that night plotting our escape. The next morning, we gratefully surrendered our fully paid rent for the remainder of the week and fled to Florence, where a new hotel gave us much appreciated refuge. We were extremely fortunate since the J&J Hotel had a rare unexpected cancellation in what was the peak of the high season for tourists like ourselves. Thoughts of the *Countessa* and our torment faded with the attentive charm of the hotel staff. We finally got to sample the delicious culinary delights of Italy. We visited the historical *Ponte Vecchio* and the *Uffizi Gallery,* to exercise the ghostly spirit of the joyless *Countessa*. We were now in the charming Italy we had heard of and that I had yet to experience.

Ageism

I've never imagined I would be the victim of ageism and certainly not under the circumstances I am about to recount. I was in Paris a few months ago on business and one evening went out with a transplanted New Yorker friend of mine for a casual drink in the Marais district. We were at a literary bar that was packed with Parisians and a few cosmopolitan English tourists out on the town. The establishment had a narrow entrance with an old fashioned mirrored bar on one side and shelves full of books on the other. The clientele was eclectic, some professional kinds but mostly writers, poets and acting types. As I stood casually against the bookshelves admiring the collection of literary works, while waiting for my buddy to return from the crowded bar with our drinks, a tall attractive woman approached me. She had that unmistakable Parisian bourgeois look about her with a twist of rebellion. She had raven hair and a couture dress draped delightfully around her tall slender Parisian frame. She stood in front of me with her arms dangling limply by her side with a cigarette in her right-hand. "Hello," she said purring like the Anglo-French actress Kristin Scott-Thomas, as she pressed against my form with her lips close and bright hazel eyes firmly fixed on mine. She seemed a bit tipsy but still in control. My guard was up. Behind her was a shorter, slightly older man that she said was her date. There were also a number of other men in their entourage who seemed to be vying for her attention. She had a good eye and appeared to have figured that I was not the average tourist in Paris. She told me she was divorced and took up with Pierre, a film director, apparently of some repute, who was a childhood family friend. This sounded typically French somehow. I could feel his eyes on me but he too seemed a little worse for wear; his speech was blurred, although he had a glass of water or perhaps absinthe in his hand and tried to portray an air of sobriety. I played French and nodded hello knowing he would be amused since a girlfriend who attracts the flirtatious attention of other men is a source of pride not offense. I may have even asked what he was working on presently. She introduced herself as Catherine and slipped me her business card. She whispered in my ear with her French sultry accent "Please call me!" And seemed disappointed when I explained I was leaving Paris the next day for London. She pondered a moment and then asked if she could have my card. I playfully said, "I don't give my card to strange women I meet at bars." She seemed to like my response.

Catherine shooed away yet another of her French admirers and returned her attention to me. She said she was a lawyer and was very rich. From the looks of her, I didn't doubt her in the least. I said, "I am afraid money does not impress me." She laughed coquettishly, and told me she was fifty. I asked her, "How old do you think I am?" she examined me very carefully, up and down for several moments and said, "Forty," to which I grinned and responded, "I am older than you." Thereafter her interest seemed to wane. It seems she was after a younger more impressionable conquest. She slipped back to Pierre, who was doubtless relieved to have her back. Her eyes followed mine as she and Pierre staggered inelegantly out of the bar.

The Overcoat

I survived one of the bleakest winters in New York history with the warmth of a spring raincoat. I'd attended a friend's raucous Christmas party downtown in the days when nobody in their right mind lived below Canal Street. It was a drunken affair full of college classmates and new arrivals to the City keen to make new friends and to party. We were all very youthful and looking for romance. I found mine with one of the hosts and ended up staying the night. I woke early, showered and searched through the pile of coats and scarves left behind for my warm lined coat. Among the mound, I found only one men's coat I could even imagine wearing; a flimsy thin ill-fitting raincoat for someone about half my size. I had no choice but to venture out clad in this strange garment with sleeves halfway up my arms and length barely beyond my *derrière*. It was bitter cold and I cursed the guest who had fled with my warm coat as I made my way to the No. 1 local subway.

Once home, I called the host for news of my errant garment. "Sorry no one has called yet," she said apologetically, "try again tomorrow." The next day I tried again and received more or less the same answer. I was freezing and desperate for my coat particularly since I could not afford a new one. My hatred for the coat thief grew with each passing winter day, as I trudged in the dark winter night through New York snow braced against the Hudson River's chilling gusts. My calls went from daily to weekly to monthly until spring finally arrived. At which point, I received a call from my friend to tell me my coat had been anonymously returned. Left at her doorstep, presumably now the coat thief had no more use for its warm protection.

ACKNOWLEDGEMENTS

Acknowledgements

I would like to thank my children for allowing me time to write once again and participating with comments and questions in our literary salons. Special thanks also to my elder brother Regi who helped jog my memory of some historic notes.

Some of the names in this book have been changed to protect the privacy of the individuals concerned but otherwise all names and events are real. I have relied on memory to recount and reconstruct events described in the book as best I can.

I received encouragement from many friends, including: Carroll Bogert, Pria Chatterjee, Adam Dixon, Bharat Dube, Jennifer Dworkin, Louis Edozien, Jenny Freeman, James E. Johnson, Beth Judy, Mde et M. Kearney (aka, Béatrice Leca and Jeffrey Kearney), Judy Levenfeld, Antonio Maldonado Camera, Anthony Maybury-Lewis, Pia Maybury-Lewis, David Pyle, Angi Triebe and my editor Anne Dubuisson Anderson. I thank you all!

Gus Udo

New York January, 2014

SUGGESTED READING

Suggested Reading

Achebe, Chinua, *The Education of a British-Protected Child*

Achebe, Chinua, *There was a Country*

Adichie, Chimamanda Ngozi, *Americanah: A Novel*

Appiah, Kwame Anthony, *Cosmopolitanism: Ethics in a World of Strangers*

Brizendine, Louann, *The Female Brain*

Conrad, Joseph, *Heart of Darkness*

Darian-Smith, Eve, *Bridging Divides: The Channel Tunnel and English Legal Identity in the New Europe*

Ehrenreich, Barbara, *The Worst Years of Our Lives: Irreverent Notes from a Decade of Greed*

Equiano, Olaudah, *Sold as a Slave*

Halpern, Daniel, edited by, *The Art of the Tale: An International Anthology of Short Stories 1945-1985*

Howkins, John, *The Creative Economy: How People Make Money from Ideas*

Huxley, Aldous, *Collected Essays*

Kahneman, Daniel, *Thinking Fast and Slow*

Kane, Cheikh Hamidou, *Ambiguous Adventure*

Lobrano Guth, Dorothy editor; revised and updated by White, Martha, *Letters of E.B. White*

Long, Sarah, *Le Dossier: How to Survive the English*

Maier, Corinne, *Bonjour Laziness: Jumping off the Corporate Ladder*

Massachusetts Committee for Children and Youth, *No Place like Home*

Orwell, George, *Down and Out in Paris and London*

Orwell, George, *Why I Write*

Sadler, Michael, *An Englishman a la Campagne: Life in Deepest France*

Sandel, Michael J., *What Money Can't Buy: The Moral Limits of Markets*

Schopenhauer, Arthur, *Essays and Aphorisms*

Steele, Claude M., *Whistling Vivaldi: How Stereotypes affect us and what we Can Do*

Stout, Martha, *The Sociopath Next Door*

Styron, William, *Darkness Visible: A Memoir of Madness*

Taylor, Craig, *Londoners*

Turnbull, Sarah, *Almost French: Love and a New Life in Paris*

White, E.B., *One Man's Meat*

Author's Biography

GUS UDO was born in Kaduna in northern Nigeria on November 16, 1959. He was raised in London and studied at Harvard College and the London School of Economics and Political Science (LSE). The author spends his time in London, Paris, and New York where he lives and works. He has two children.

This is the author's second book. He is currently working on a third, a book of children's stories.

www.ingramcontent.com/pod-product-compliance
Lightning Source LLC
Chambersburg PA
CBHW020912090426
42736CB00008B/598